Reimagining Business Education

Insights and Actions from the
Business Education Jam

Reimagining Business Education

Insights and Actions from the Business Education Jam

By

Paul R. Carlile
Steven H. Davidson
Kenneth W. Freeman
Howard Thomas
N. Venkatraman

*Boston University Questrom School of Business
Boston, Massachusetts, USA*

Emerald

United Kingdom – North America – Japan
India – Malaysia – China

Emerald Group Publishing Limited
Howard House, Wagon Lane, Bingley BD16 1WA, UK

First edition 2016

British Library Cataloguing in Publication Data
A catalogue record for this book is available from the British Library

ISBN: 978-1-78635-368-9

INVESTOR IN PEOPLE

Contents

About the Authors

Paul R. Carlile is Associate Professor of Management and the Senior Associate Dean for Innovation at the Boston University Questrom School of Business. He was previously at the MIT Sloan School of Management and also served as Department Chair of Information Systems at the Boston University Questrom School of Business. Dr. Carlile's research focuses on the boundaries that exist among people in different knowledge domains and what can be done to address them in order to enhance collaboration and innovative outcomes. He has helped develop ways to enhance collaboration and innovation in the automotive, software, aerospace, pharmaceutical, and educational industries. Dr. Carlile's work as Senior Associate Dean for Innovation has focused on enhancement of student learning through curricular innovation and new models of program delivery, including the new launch of the integrated and experientially based MS in Management Studies (MSMS) Program, cited as a Most Innovative Business School Idea of 2015 by *Poets & Quants*. Dr. Carlile holds a BA in Philosophy and Masters in Organizational Behavior from Brigham Young University, and a PhD in Organizational Behavior from the University of Michigan.

Steven H. Davidson is Associate Dean, Academic Programs, at Boston University Questrom School of Business and served as the lead Project Manager for the Business Education Jam. In his role as Associate Dean, Steven provides leadership for cross-program efforts including assessment, program research, accreditation, and the development, support, and implementation of curricular initiatives, program enhancements, and academic policy. Steven previously worked in areas including graduate admission, program administration, learning assessment, and was previously Assistant Dean for Strategic

Initiatives & Student Learning. Steven holds a BS in Decision Sciences and Management Information Systems from George Mason University, an Ed.M. in Administration Training & Policy Studies from Boston University, and is nearing completion of a Doctorate in Educational Leadership and Development at Boston University School of Education, with primary interests in accreditation, program development, and supporting curricular innovation.

Kenneth W. Freeman joined Boston University as the Allen Questrom Professor and Dean of the Questrom School of Business in 2010. Ken has more than 40 years of professional experience, most recently at KKR where he was a partner and also served as a senior advisor. He is vice chairman of the Graduate Management Admission Council, a member of the AACSB Committee on Issues in Management Education and the Business Practices Council, and Chairman of the Board of Trustees of Bucknell University. Ken began his career at Corning Incorporated in 1972, progressing through the financial function before leading several businesses. He joined Corning Clinical Laboratories in 1995, and the company was spun off from Corning as Quest Diagnostics Incorporated soon thereafter. He led the dramatic turnaround of Quest Diagnostics as chairman and chief executive officer through 2004. A study of global business leadership conducted at INSEAD and published in the January 2013 issue of the Harvard Business Review named Ken one of the 100 best performing CEOs in the world. Ken holds a BS in Business Administration from Bucknell University, and an MBA with Distinction from Harvard Business School.

Howard Thomas is the LKCSB Distinguished Professor of Strategic Management, Lee Kong Chian School of Business, Director of the Academic Strategy and Management Education Unit, Singapore Management University, and the inaugural Ahmass Fakahany Distinguished Visiting Professor at Boston University Questrom School of Business. A highly cited scholar, Dr. Thomas holds fellowship awards including the U.S. Academy of Management, the British Academy of Management, the Strategic Management Society, the Academy of Social Sciences, and the Institute of Directors. He is a companion of the Association of Business Schools, former board chair of the Graduate Management Admissions Council (GMAC), AACSB International, the Association of Business Schools (ABS), and the Global Foundation of Management Education (GFME). Dr. Thomas is also an honorary life member and a board member of the European Foundation for Management Development (EFMD) and has had Deanships and Senior Administrative positions at London Business School, AGSM, the University of Illinois at Urbana-Champaign, Warwick Business School, and Singapore Management University. Dr. Thomas hold a B.Sc. and M.Sc. in Statistics from London University, an MBA from University of Chicago, PhD in Decision Analysis and D.Sc. from Edinburgh University, and is the recipient of several honorary degrees.

N. Venkatraman is the David J. McGrath, Jr. Professor in Management at Boston University Questrom School of Business. He was previously at the MIT Sloan School and London Business School, and also served as Department Chair of Information Systems and Faculty Director, MSMBA Program, at Boston University School Questrom of Business. Dr. Venkatraman was awarded the 2004 and 2006 IBM Faculty Fellowship for his work focusing on business challenges in the network era. His research and teaching lie at the interface between strategic management and information technology with a particular focus on how companies position to win in a network era. Dr. Venkatraman's current research includes information technology strategy, design and management of interfirm relationships through information technology, globalization through information technology, structural equation models, and second generation network research methods. Dr. Venkatraman holds a B. Tech degree from IIT Kharagpur, an MBA from IIM Calcutta, and PhD from University of Pittsburgh.

Acknowledgments

The Business Education Jam started with an idea – to bring the world together for a first of its kind comprehensive dialogue about the future of business education with participation of all stakeholders – academia, industry, government, and beyond. This idea would not have become a reality without the inspiring collaborative and global engagement which occurred before, during, and after the Business Education Jam.

A remarkable group of organizations, volunteers, and colleagues dedicated their time, ideas, and energy to make the Business Education Jam a reality. In particular, the authors extend gratitude to the IBM Innovation Jam Team, led by Liam Cleaver, Vice President, Social Insight Group. They guided the almost yearlong process from idea to reality and remained committed to our goals of an open, engaging brainstorm. We thank the many faculty and scholars, including those within the Questrom School of Business, who helped to refine the content and approach of the Jam. We are grateful to the nearly 100 volunteers and area leads who guided Jam development and facilitated the 60 consecutive hour conversation between September 30 and October 2, 2014. They were the backbone of the effort.

The Business Education Jam was purposefully designed as a highly collaborative process and the extensive engagement of the Jam's many supporters made it possible. We thank the Jam sponsors who provided initial encouragement, advice, and important financial resources, including our presenting sponsors – Boston University Questrom School of Business, GMAC, Johnson & Johnson, Merck, and the Financial Times; our collaboration sponsors – AACSB International, EFMD, IBM, Santander, and the Boston University Questrom School of Business Human Resources Policy Institute; and our partners – EY, Fidelity Investments, and PwC. We also extend our deep gratitude and appreciation to the 99 VIP Guests and Hosts who dedicated their time and talent to provide valuable insights which shaped the global conversation.

In particular, we thank several individuals for their advice, collaboration, and encouragement during the Jam development process: Dan LeClair, Executive Vice President and Chief Operating Officer at AACSB International; Matthew Wood, Director of Operations at EFMD; Sangeet Chowfla, President and CEO of the Graduate Management Admission Council (GMAC), and the members of the AACSB Business Practices Council. Each provided invaluable guidance and were willing to join us in taking the risk by embracing such a global and unprecedented event. We are also grateful to Michael J. Arena, Chief Talent Officer, General Motors Corporation, for contributing an insightful prescript to this book; and to Jeffrey Pfeffer, Thomas D. Dee II Professor of Organizational Behavior, Graduate School of Business, Stanford University, for contributing a postscript which encourages us to challenge ourselves even further.

Finally, we thank the many scholars, deans, faculty, students, staff, and members of industry who have used the Jam findings to inform their own work and are collectively driving forward educational innovations and encourage others to join us in taking the next step in reimagining business education. This book is much more than a summary of the Business Education Jam. It is about much more than challenges. We have tremendous opportunities as we reimagine business education. We applaud the many schools that have adopted the findings of the Jam as their call to action, and encourage continued, collaborative dialogue across all stakeholders as we proceed to ensure the relevance, reach, and respect of the business education models of the future.

Prescript: Reimagining Business Schools

Business school education has historically been an essential element in driving business performance and growth. The symbiotic relationship between organizations and business schools has resulted in economic development, business success, and graduate achievement. However, more recently, there is a growing divide between academia and business. While scholarly research and theory, first argued for by a 1959 report funded by the Ford Foundation, served its purpose for decades, times have shifted. The publish-or-perish dictum has generated a chasm between business theory and practice. The pendulum has swung too far in the other direction since the mid-20th century. Ironically, the need for practice-based research has perhaps never been greater.

Today, businesses face an unprecedented level of complexity and change. Global economic pressures, rapidly evolving technology, radical connectivity, and a dynamic competitive landscape have fundamentally amplified business uncertainties. Entire industries are poised for disruption. Consider the average life expectancy of a company in the S&P 500 index; in 1957 a business had a life expectancy of 75 years. Currently, businesses last only for 15 years (Kuhlmann, 2010). In the midst of such complexities, there is a demand for relevant research and adaptive practices. Yet, most business schools are missing in action.

The divide isn't limited to practice-theory; there is also a skills challenge with graduating students entering into business. Business schools are well aware of some of the more chronic gaps, such as professional writing skills, business model innovation, and analytics. However, the escalation of complexity has ushered in new, emerging needs. There's a greater need for graduates to understand internal social dynamics and critical thinking to enable adaptation in response to a rapidly changing business world. While content is increasingly becoming a commodity, with the rise of MOOCs (massive open online courses), Google and YouTube, individuals have access to real-time knowledge on an as-needed basis, the judgment of knowing when, where, and how to leverage such information is increasingly important. Skills such as business judgment, social awareness, and critical thinking aren't gained through conventional lectures, papers, and exams but through experiential learning and practice. This requires active partnerships between business schools and businesses.

Academia seems to be caught up in its own impending demise. Escalating tuition cost, declining placement rates, the rise of distance-learning, and the entry of non-traditional competition, have hijacked university focus. For the first time in academic history the cost-benefit ratio of traditional education is being debated. Exacerbating the divide even further is the obsession for faculty tenure that doesn't reward business practice experience and is preoccupied with growingly obscure research that is worthy of A-level journal publication. The self-perpetuating aspects of academia and the doubling-down of ineffective practices within organizations have resulted in a partnership divide. Each has entered into a new normal, creating a polarization of business practice and business education.

To shift direction, one must first shift the conversation. That is exactly what *Reimagining Business Education* does. The Business Education Jam: Envisioning the Future explicitly articulates the key challenges and then provides a bridge to facilitate real conversation. The Business Education Jam engaged thousands of people in a massive on-line discussion, debate, and practical dialogue around the future of business education. Key stakeholders included faculty, deans, and administrators, business executives, hiring managers, students, and graduates. By engaging the whole system in an open exchange of ideas, new insights emerged. The Business Education Jam followed the structure of Think Big, Start Small, and Scale Fast. Starting with the grand challenge of envisioning the future of business education, then exchanging thousands of small ideas with actionable solutions that can be evaluated and iterated, with successful ideas being scaled across and within institutions.

In the end, Reimagining Business Schools will be a journey rather than merely a one-time exchange. The journey will require a curriculum that is more closely aligned with the practical demands of today's employers, a curriculum that anticipates and addresses tomorrow's challenges. This transformative journey will also require active partnerships between academia and businesses that encourage on-going experiential learning. The journey will drive more practice-based research. Finally, it will require a mixture of scholarly researchers and seasoned practitioners who co-create new theories and practices. Reimagining Business Schools provides the framework to launch this journey, making business education more relevant, accessible, and actionable.

Michael J. Arena
Chief Talent Officer, General Motors Corporation

1

The Need for Real Innovation in Business Education

Business schools teach innovation but themselves rarely innovate. Rather, they remain stuck in approaches to business education that have changed very little for more than half a century. It has been described as "an industry that, if not actually in crisis, is certainly suffering from a bad case of existential angst" (Thomas, Lorange, & Sheth, 2013).

Certainly, some tinkering at the margins has occurred: course offerings have been diversified somewhat; flexible or alternative delivery formats for MBA programs have been introduced; program durations have been compressed; specialized masters programs have proliferated; and technology has made some inroads into the classroom.

However, these developments have largely involved replication and reinforcement of long-standing approaches to business education. Genuine innovation – in instruction, in content, in research, in partnerships with business, and in the b-school business model itself – remains the exception.

As a result, stakeholders in business education – students, employers, governments, expert commentators, funding agencies, and potential donors – now seriously question its value and impact. For example, as noted by Thomas et al. (2013, p. 54) *Financial Times* journalist Skapinker (2011) points out that few people pay attention to management research because it is irrelevant and does not engage with management practices. In a similar vein Bennis and O'Toole (2005) ask why "business schools have embraced the scientific model of physicists and economists rather than the professional model of doctors and lawyers."

While the rest of the world innovates at a furious pace in almost every area of human endeavor, business and management education continues to drift on the tide of past success. Now that tide is going out. Unless we as an "industry" find innovative ways to change our path and provide greater value to students, employers, and the world at large, today's drift will become tomorrow's full-blown crisis of legitimacy.

Tinkering will not get us through. We will need comprehensive innovation and we will need everyone to lend a hand to make it happen.

That is what this book is about.

It is a dialogue intended to provoke and speed the process of innovation by involving as many stakeholders as possible. The aim is to open business education to innovation and radical change – and to do this through leveraging open innovation – before the world leaves business education behind.

How did we arrive in our current situation?

In the late 1950s two seminal American reports on business education, one commissioned by the Ford Foundation and the other by the Carnegie Foundation, called for business schools to adopt a stronger academic approach to the teaching of business (Gordon & Howell, 1959; Pierson, 1959).

The aim was to elevate the status of these burgeoning institutions through skill-centered curricula, research approaches mimicking the sciences, and widely accepted standards of accreditation. Thus was ushered in a "golden age" of business education. Enrollment boomed, business schools thrived, and the MBA degree became the golden ticket to success.

By the beginning of the 21st century, however, that model of business education had begun to lose its relevance in a greatly changed and globalized world. In the years that followed, the age-old fissure between academia and the outside world became a chasm.

inform their own strategic efforts to transform or engage with business education. Recent presentations we have been invited to make at conferences sponsored by AACSB, EFMD, and GMAC demonstrate the intense desire of business school deans to make positive changes to support the needs of employers and ensure the relevance of their own institutions in today's global economy.

This global dialogue will continue as the Questrom School of Business engages collaboratively to identify the next steps in bridging the interests of academia and industry, including AACB'S visioning initiative, webinars in collaboration with the *Financial Times*, EMFD and GMAC research and conference activities, and the launching of additional open platform events with expanded global participation.

> Like any mature industry, ours needs shaking up. If business schools look the same in 10 years as they do now, many will be out of business – or at least deserve to be out of business.

Why did Boston University Questrom School of Business decide to take the risk to spearhead this unique global effort? We did so not only because we believed such a conversation was long overdue and sorely needed but also because we saw it as a logical outgrowth of our school's history of innovation.

Among the oldest business schools in the world, Questrom School of Business was one of the first to admit women, to establish an MBA program, and to institute specific curricula addressing nonprofit and health care management.

We created the Center for Team Learning and the first MS-MBA, a high-tech dual-degree merging technology with business needs. We taught entrepreneurial studies before it had a formal name. We pioneered the move from the operations and financially based management models of the past into the network-centric curricula of today.

In September 2013, we marked our 100th anniversary as the Boston University School of Management and in March 2015 became the Boston University Questrom School of Business as a result of a transformative gift by Allen and Kelli Questrom and their foundation.

Allen, class of 1964, is a first-generation graduate whose professional trajectory was dramatically and positively affected by his education at the school, then known as the College of Business Administration. We saw our centennial as a reason to look forward rather than looking back, and under our new name we intend to continue to break new ground.

This book is yet another step in that direction.

Whether you are affiliated with a business school, an organization that hires business school graduates, a think tank, a funding agency, or a media organization that follows business education, you should find much of interest here.

This book provides a strong case for reimagining business education.

Chapter 2 identifies critical challenges gathered from relevant literature which informed the development of the Jam.

Chapter 3 then examines the Jam development process and how its uniquely collaborative and external-facing design enabled a global conversation.

Then, in Chapter 4, we build on these design principles as we address the emerging impact of open innovation – the animating principle of the Jam and its role as a powerful tool for gathering and analyzing advanced ideas in a world where knowledge is widely distributed.

Chapter 5 examines the critical gaps between theory and practice which are increasing the tension between industry and business education.

Chapter 6 then explores how business education can be reimagined and offers meaningful scenarios and ideas for change.

Finally, the book concludes with an examination of potential next steps for this global dialogue.

Our hope is that after reading this you, whether an administrator or faculty member in a business school, an executive in industry, a student, an alumnus, or a public policy official, will actively take up the cause of constructive change for business education.

Like any mature industry, ours needs shaking up. If business schools look the same in 10 years as they do now, many will be out of business – or at least deserve to be out of business.

We cannot afford complacency. The Business Education Jam has launched a compelling movement toward a more innovative and collaborative future for business education.

However, no single institution, association, or educator can do it alone and much work remains to be done. We need to enlarge the "crowd" to include stakeholders in emerging economies, add government and NGO voices to those of academia and industry, and open largely "western" perspectives to other points of view.

We need to put to work some of the wisdom that has already been synthesized: innovative and effective ways to bridge the gap between business schools and industry, meet the higher expectations of employers and students, and create standards that reward creativity over conformity.

Above all, we must innovate together if we are to achieve relevance, reach, and respect that will not just see us through the current crisis but also usher in the next exciting transformation (and perhaps even a new golden age) of business education.

2 Critical Challenges

2.1. Introduction

The Ford and Carnegie reports (Gordon & Howell, 1959; Pierson, 1959) significantly impacted the model of management education. These reports moved management education from what Simon (1997) and Augier and March (2011, p. 28) described as "wastelands of vocationalism" (essentially a "trade school" orientation) into a "science-based model" with a focus on analysis and discipline-oriented thinking.

This logical, positivist paradigm came to dominate the business school educational model as deans sought to create both academic legitimacy and a clearer identity for business schools. Standards for research were raised, programs were evaluated to ensure sufficient academic content, and business schools elevated their reputation for rigor and quality.

In the new millennium, however, this model became the focus of intense criticism. Academia began to examine the academic content and research quality of management education, while industry stakeholders simultaneously voiced concerns about the relevance of research and its impact to practice. And students began to increasingly question the value of attending business school given the ever increasing price tag and questionable economic return.

As we sought to re-imagine future pathways for business and management education, we reviewed the literature and writings on management education to identify critical questions and ongoing challenges. These critical questions would begin to serve as a framework for the process of creating, structuring, and engaging in the Business Education Jam. The set of questions outlined below became an initial organizational framework used to engage stakeholders in early dialogue on creating the Business Education Jam.

2.2. Critical Questions

1. The Global Mindset

How can management education create value in a globalized world in which there is a trade-off between globalization and local or regional differentiation – the "globalization effect"? (Fraguiero, 2010, p. 184)

As Thomas, Lee, Thomas, and Wilson (2014, p. 186) wrote: "there is a prevailing sense that we generally do not know how to inculcate global skills in our students or incorporate [them] in our curricula."

> The problem with business schools is that disruptive technology is met with inertia, conservatism, and a lack of willingness to change

We therefore need to examine the balance between the challenges of globalization and the importance of establishing local and regional identity in our business schools.

2. The Relevance Deficit

How should we address the perception of the increasing irrelevance and minimal impact of business school research on the management community? How can business schools' management research drive insights for business, government, and industry?

Pfeffer and Fong (2002, 2004) argue that business schools have been ineffective in creating useful business ideas. And Beer (2001) believes that schools – with their unerring focus on A-journal research – produce research that cannot be implemented.

3.   The Disruptive Deficit

How will technology continue to challenge the model of business education?

Christensen and Eyring's (2011) book on the innovative university addresses the impacts of disruptive e-learning technologies on teaching pedagogy and research.

The problem with business schools is that disruptive technology (e.g., MOOCs, on-line blended learning) is met with inertia, conservatism, and a lack of willingness to change. In addition, as Tett (*Financial Times*, 2013) points out, "these (technological) trends have the potential to devastate universities" economic models. If students can now download a course on their iPad anywhere in the world, they might question whether they need to attend an elite college at all."

4.   The Reputation Game: Pandering to the Rankings

How will policy, accreditation, and rankings influence the development of business education and business?

It is clear that business schools have accepted market and institutional forces as determinants of educational quality "through their relatively unquestioned acceptance of accreditations, rankings, league tables, student satisfaction surveys, and individual and corporate donations" (Thomas, Lorange, & Sheth, 2013, p. 68).

Further, Khurana (2007) identifies the "tyranny of the rankings" that can lead to dysfunctional managerial choices in business schools as they seek to manage rankings and league tables rather than investment in teaching and research excellence (Thomas et al., 2013, p. 68).

5.   The Leadership Skills Deficit: Values-Based Leadership

How can academia and industry collaborate to ensure students have critical leadership skills and management competencies?

Mintzberg (2004) has been the most zealous critic of schools that focus too much on teaching specialist analytical skills and not giving significant attention to management and leadership abilities. He believes that management is an art or craft and not a science, a practice involving soft skills and experience blended with careful vision and insight and enriched by appropriate analytic tools to achieve sound managerial decisions.

He identifies five frames, or themes, which address the practice of management in a holistic way:

- The *reflective mindset* (leadership, emotional intelligence, and so on)
- The *collaborative mindset* (alliances, teams)
- The *analytic mindset* (theoretical approaches to decision making)
- The *worldly mindset* (globalization, cultural intelligence)
- The *action mindset* (managing change and growth)

These five frames should be augmented systematically by appropriate treatment of operational excellence and value creation.

Ultimately, as Turpin (2013) notes, authentic leadership and personal skills and values make the leadership difference.

6.   The Change Mindset

How will government and industry tap the potential of millennials?

The time is ripe for change in management education, but any change is likely to face the drag of conservatism and organizational inertia.

Faculty in business schools are often content with their more discipline-focused and theoretical research-oriented recipes for business schools success. As a consequence, not only deans but their faculties are seen as both resistant to change and impeding business model innovation. (Thomas et al., 2014, p. 42)

This can be seen, for example, in the pedagogy of business schools. Millennial students embrace new learning technologies and experiential, action-based learning but many faculty are still more comfortable with the "sage on the stage" model of lecturing to students. For many incumbent business school professors, escaping from the past is often difficult.

There is clearly a need, therefore, for a paradigm shift and for creating alternative models that better reflect technology learning styles and the need for a truly global outlook.

7.   The Humanistic Deficit

How can ethical leadership be fostered across business education and industry?

It is often argued, particularly since the global financial crisis of 2007/2008, that business schools do not provide a clear sense of purpose, morality, and ethics with respect to thier role in society.

In an important article (2005), the late Sumantra Ghoshal wrote: "I suggest that by perpetuating ideologically inspired amoral theories, business schools have actively freed their students from any sense of moral responsibility."

Corporate scandals, often attributed to CEOs trained in business schools (Thomas et al., 2013, p. 67), such as those at World.Com or Enron and more recently at a range of financial institutions, merely add to the view that the business school's ethical, moral, and societal conscience can be summarized as "greed is good."

8.   The Entrepreneurship/Innovation Deficit

What roles should business schools play in developing the next generation of entrepreneurs and innovators?

Thomas et al. (2014, p. 178) note that one common theme is the rhetoric about studying the entrepreneurship gap and the value of studying entrepreneurship, but there is almost nothing about how to implement this into the norms and curricula topics of business schools. They suggest that the niche contributions to entrepreneurship education advanced by some specialist schools should be more studied and integrated into mainstream business school curricula.

9.   The Governance Deficit

How can the often difficult relationship between the business school and its parent institution (most often a university) be improved?

The uneasy positioning of the business school in the modern university and the tension between the business school and its university are increasingly evident.

Derek Bok, former President of Harvard University, notes that "among the faculties none has a greater sense of purpose than the business school" (Bok, 2003, p. 76). Yet Bloom (1987) charges business schools with contributing to the excessive commercialization of universities. He stresses that "the MBA is not the mark of the scholarly achievement ... motivated by the love of the science of economics but by love of what it is concerned with – money."

This uneasy tension and ambiguous positioning means that the autonomy granted to business schools in the past may be eroding as university governance is increasingly enforced upon them. Thus, it would appear that the role, acceptance, and legitimacy of business schools within academia is increasingly being questioned.

10.   The Financial Sustainability Deficit

How can schools identify innovative solutions to recast their business and financial models more effectively and appropriately?

The funding of business schools and the sustainability of current financial models are increasingly pressing issues. Business schools face growing pressure on both the revenue and cost sides of their financial models and have already suffered declines in public funding as a consequence of the global financial crisis and radical views about higher education being more a private than a public good (Peters & Thomas, 2011; Thomas & Peters, 2012).

> "I suggest that by perpetuating ideologically inspired amoral theories, business schools have actively freed their students from any sense of moral responsibility"
>
> Sumantra Ghoshal (2005)

An escalation of tuition costs for the traditional cash-cow EMBA and MBA programs is unlikely to be sustainable. Also, income from executive education programs and donations are not stable nor are they within reach of all business schools.

Indeed, Peters and Thomas (2011) note that the high-cost faculty model is potentially unsustainable. Faculty costs account for the lion's share of a school's expenditure, with the upward trend in salaries driven in part by a demand-supply gap. "How long can this go on?" is a recurring question in the minds of business school leaders and the need for more innovative and flexible structures is clear.

2.3. Conclusion

Management education is at a crossroads. And given uncertain futures, we need to examine the strengths of business schools, how they have evolved, and how they can increase their relevance, reach, and respect. What is the future roadmap of management education? How will business schools increase their impact on practice? How will they meet shifting employer needs? How will we cater to the new generations of students? How will we nurture and grow the leaders of the future?

These are key questions the Jam sought to answer.

3 Enabling a Global Conversation – The Business Education Jam

C hapters 1 and 2 highlighted a number of critical questions facing business schools, particularly the increasing view that business schools are not innovating but appear "stuck in approaches to business education that have changed very little for more than half a century" and that there is a need for "stronger partnerships with industry."

These two themes, among others, began to frame the design of the Business Education Jam. As the first event of its kind in business education, the outcome of the Jam was uncertain but the design was purposeful. Building off the imperative for the Jam discussed in Chapters 1 and 2, this chapter will provide context on the design of the Jam and the challenges of creating such an outward-facing global dialogue. Many of these challenges will subsequently resonate with the concepts of an open platform discussed in Chapter 4.

3.1. Recognizing the Need for a Global Dialogue

The Questrom School of Business has always placed a high priority on ensuring effective, impactful, rigorous academic programs. However, like most business schools, program innovations while positive were often modest and reflected improvements of existing educational models, not the creation of new ones. This began to change in the Fall of 2011 with the creation of two school wide committees tasked with undertaking the most substantial review of curricula in more than 15 years. The work of these two committees led to design changes for two of the most significant programs in the school: the undergraduate BSBA program, a four-year program with 2,500 students, and the full-time MBA, a two-year program with 300 students.

These activities represented the beginning of an ongoing dialogue that asked "Are we doing enough to innovate across our academic programs and meet emerging employer demands?" The rapid growth of the global economy, changing business needs, and emerging student trends made it increasingly clear that program reform needed to be a continual process and that we must question the *status quo* apparent in our industry.

In 2013, as curriculum changes were being implemented, the Questrom School of Business celebrated is centennial as one of the oldest business schools in the world. As part of this, the Dean of Questrom, along with leading Questrom faculty, began to engage more broadly outside the school to ask "How are we, as an industry, responding to the incredibly rapid changes surrounding us?" And, importantly, "How must business education evolve to meet these changes?" The feedback received from many business school deans and members of industry was that, yes, change was needed. However, as an industry the business school roadmap to a successful future was not clear.

This desire to engage in a meaningful and far-reaching conversation on the future of business education then led to IBM, which with its Jam technology had a proven technology platform and methodology for scaling a global brainstorm and extracting key themes and findings. In Fall 2013, conceptual conversations with IBM led to a commitment to move forward on the Business Education Jam with a tentative March 2014 launch date.

The IBM Jam technology had proven to be a powerful tool for engagement and has been used by more than 100 leading companies and global organizations to drive positive change. Conversations with past Jam participants and sponsoring executives revealed the experiences and effectiveness of the technology. The results were clear: organizations consistently reported a positive, meaningful experience from the Jam. While each approached the Jam differently, all found it broke down silos, encouraged dialogue, helped their organization culturally, and led to new, implementable ideas or products. However, two concepts on how to design the Business Education Jam quickly emerged.

First, there needed to be an early plan on how ideas, comments, and themes generated during the Jam were to be used after the Jam concluded. Organizations that had taken part in previous Jams were often surprised, and in some cases partially overwhelmed, with the number of ideas and comments generated during their Jam. In one case, a financial firm had promised in advance of its Jam that organizational leadership would respond to every suggested new idea for a product or service improvement. This resulted, following the Jam, in needing the equivalent of one full-time staff member to manage the process. Other organizations found it difficult to articulate concrete next steps as opposed to a broad summary of concepts. To avoid such potential issues, the Business Education Jam team deliberately designed the Jam to spark actionable, implementable ideas and not just a high-level summary of timeworn and previously discussed ideas. The goal of this was to enable rapid production of a concluding report and findings.

The second conclusion from these conversations was of great importance. Historically, Jams have focused inwardly, on a captive audience, with limited insights emanating from outside the corporation or organization. Most corporate-based Jams, and the only other Jam conducted by a University (the Unijam held by the University of South Australia in 2013) purposefully focused on defined populations, such as current employees, students, or alumni. These populations each have a more intimate relationship with the organizer of the Jam which increases the likelihood of participation and at the same time limits the creation of new ideas. Senior executives were often involved in the Jams, which made some within the organization feel there was a requirement to participate, even though no such requirement existed. Other Jams, such as the Habitat Jam hosted by the Government of Canada, UN-Habitat, and IBM, did include external engagement, but none with the breadth the Business Education Jam envisioned. Engaging an external audience – and ensuring they actually participate in the Jam – presents a unique set of challenges. *This need to ensure the Business Education Jam be constructed outwardly, to engage a broad audience, would become a defining characteristic of the Jam development process.*

3.2. Establishing Support

After the decision to utilize IBM Jam technology was made, a small team of faculty and staff within the Questrom School of Business was formed to work directly with the IBM team to facilitate the creation of the Business Education Jam requirements. IBM, with its deep experience in leading Jams, could clearly articulate Jam requirements and had a formalized process and timeline to ensure readiness for the Jam. This included weekly conference calls with a dedicated IBM team, establishment of project milestones, development of marketing, content, and research plans, and the utilization of IBM-developed templates to align content for the Jam.

To structure engagement with IBM, work areas were created in alignment with traditional IBM Jam designs. Each area would be initially led by a faculty or staff member from the Questrom School of Business and included:

- *Project and Event Management*: A lead project manager worked across all Jam leadership areas, serving as a central point of contact for IBM and was responsible for ensuring all Jam deliverables were completed.

- *Marketing and Communications*: A team was established to provide leadership for all Jam communications, ensuring consistent messaging, marketing plans, and a social media strategy. Unlike most other organizational Jams, the Business Education Jam had a more significant focus on external communication given the wide stakeholder engagement desired.
- *Event Facilitation*: To ensure adequate support during the Jam, a separate team focused on event logistics and facilitation requirements during the Jam.

Beyond these traditional roles, the aspirations of the Business Education Jam required a design that would effectively engage a wide variety of external stakeholders. After examining past Jams and in collaboration with IBM, several work areas were uniquely structured for the Business Education Jam to ensure an exceptional level of outward facing interactions. These newly established roles included:

- *Development and Outreach*: The Jam would not be feasible without the support of external organizations to assist in financial, intellectual, and outreach efforts. The Jam project manager, leading faculty, corporate relations staff, and development staff all coordinated closely on the engagement of external organizations to solicit feedback on the design of the Jam and to procure funding.
- *VIP Engagement*: The 99 VIPs and hosts who engaged in this transformational conversation came from industry, academia, and the non-profit sectors across the globe. Virtually none had participated in a Jam before and each viewed the challenges facing business education through a different lens. To effectively meet their needs and facilitate their engagement, an Assistant Project Manager was established as a formal VIP liaison.
- *On-Campus Events*: While Jams are a virtual activity, the Business Education Jam invited individuals from around the world to participate on site in Boston. In addition, given the unique setting of a university campus there was an exceptional opportunity to engage students, faculty, alumni, and corporate guests face-to-face on site during the Jam.

- *Research*: While all Jams inherently involve research before, during, and after the Jam, the research requirements of the Business Education Jam required a level of heightened collaborative engagement. Traditional factors that could influence future research, such as the establishment of registration parameters, could not be developed in a silo but needed engagement across faculty, Jam leadership, and outside stakeholders.
- *Content*: Unlike most Jams, where the basis of content is driven by internal stakeholders, the breadth of the Business Education Jam required a strong focus on external engagement to shape the final topics.

Each of these new focus areas did not emerge overnight. They were created as the unique requirements of the Business Education Jam evolved. Across all the areas of Jam development, content and external engagement consumed the greatest amount of time and attention.

3.3. Advancing an Outward-Facing Design

With the support structure for the Jam still in its infancy, consisting of just a Project Manager and a few Questrom faculty, initial conversations began externally with stakeholders to ask "Should we collectively engage in this global brainstorm?" and if so, "What should be the outcomes?" Those questions would form the basis of a cascading set of dialogues that continually expanded the Jams reach, created excitement for the potential impact of the Jam, and enhanced its design long before the event began.

First, initial dialogues began with industry to explore the perceived disconnect between academic leaders and industry executives on whether graduate competencies meet employers' needs. A presentation prepared for members of industry in January 2014 positioned the need for industry engagement as follows:

- Corporations intimately understand their employees, the challenges their company faces, and the skills required of new hires. The **perspective and needs of corporations will drive the conversation** forward.

- Corporate **engagement can occur on many levels**, including the use of corporate VIP hosts to seed conversation, employee participation in the Jam at any organizational level, and the influencing of Jam topics.
- Corporations ensure **their voice** is heard and will be positioned at the **leading edge of a global conversation.**
- Corporations will have **direct exposure** to leading business schools, faculty, thought leaders, students – and future employees.
- The value does not stay in the Jam – participants will be exposed to new ideas, networks, and innovations that can be brought back for **exploration or implementation within their organization.**

These initial conversations with industry representatives, from recruiters to executives, were well received. There was recognition by employers of changing business needs which requires a well-prepared work force and an appetite to engage more holistically with business schools. Of the employers who had utilized a Jam within their own organizations, there was an additional level of excitement and interest for the potential of the Business Education Jam.

To begin to engage business education more broadly as an industry, the Jam team captured the energy and insights gained from conversations with executives and began to engage several leading organizations helping to shape the future of management education including AACSB International, EFMD, and GMAC. The desire of early dialogue with these impactful and influential organizations was to assess their reaction to the need for a global dialogue on this topic, consider if the Jam could help to facilitate this dialogue, explore how they could assist in the Jam development process, engage their membership in the Jam process, and potentially utilize Jam findings for their own efforts.

The conversations with each organization led to initial agreement that there did exist opportunities in business education and that a global conversation – particularly one with industry – could help usher in a new era of reimagining business education. The initial tagline for the Jam then emerged in

January 2014, as "The future of business education has never before been discussed in a comprehensive, collaborative, global forum by all stakeholders ... until now."

With the support of industry and business education organizations, the dialogue then moved towards academia. Using existing networks, faculty and business school deans from across the world began to be consulted on how we could collectively engage in this envisioned Jam. Although there was some initial skepticism, leading scholars and teachers voiced support for this new and innovative idea. To test the concept of the Jam, the Questrom School of Business held an internal "mini-Jam" in January 2014 attended by nearly all full-time faculty of the school. The purpose of this on-site activity was to explore and shape potential content for the Jam. The reaction was overwhelming, with faculty expressing enthusiasm to engage in dialogue, share ideas, and seek out new ways to drive management education forward.

The conversations with industry and academic stakeholders were critical in shaping the goals and design of the Jam, and in late January 2014 the initial positioning of the Jam emerged as follows:

> The world is changing and so must business education. How will global disruptive forces impact faculty, students, research, curricula, industry needs, and the perceived value of a business education? What is the role of business schools moving forward? Although there are both dire predictions and innovative responses to these questions, one thing is clear — there is no agreed upon answer. Business school leaders, faculty, employers, and industry must consider how new technology, emerging educational models, and shifting employer needs will impact their engagement with business education.

External interest in the Jam continued to grow and the Jam project team recognized, in late January 2014, that the initial launch date of March 2014 was too restrictive. If the team was to successfully design the Jam in a collaborative nature, drawing on external insights and building a robust portfolio of VIP guests, it would need more time. The decision was made to move the Jam to the end of September 2014. This would provide time for essential external engagements to take place while avoiding the traditionally busy time of early September when North American business schools begin their fall semesters. Later dates were avoided as the end of the year increased the likelihood of conflicts for both industry and academics.

Following the establishment of the new dates priority focus was placed on two areas of external engagement: creating formalized sponsorships of the Jam and collaboratively refining Jam content with a broad set of stakeholders.

Most Jams have a primary sponsor who supports the development of the Jam financially and conceptually. For the Business Education Jam the Questrom School of Business was the primary driving force. However, it needed the support of other organizations both to offset the financial cost and provide additional validity of the effort. First, corporations that had expressed a high interest in the Jam were approached over possible financial sponsorship. The Business Education Jam needed strong industry partners to guide the Jam's efforts to effectively engage industry on a broad scale. It quickly emerged that while industry partners would be willing to contribute financially, they also wanted to be engaged on a more holistic level by contributing to content, understanding how the Jam was designed, and exploring findings.

Fidelity Investments, a Jam sponsor, undertook an active role in seeking to understand the Jam design and how it could be leveraged to impact an organization. PwC, another Jam sponsor, provided impactful insights for Jam content through its existing research, some of which was featured on the Jam portal homepage. Soliciting industry sponsorship presented a unique challenge as it soon emerged that most grant or award cycles were complete for the year. Despite this, the Business Education Jam felt so "different" to industry members that they understood its potential impact and were able to secure resources to support it. Overall, the number of firms solicited for engagement resulted in several strong, fully committed corporate partners.

The focus then turned to key academic organizations in business education – AACSB International, EFMD, and GMAC. Each organization had already contributed to the Jam conceptually and the dialogue continued to examine potential contributions to the Jam process including time, resources, and expertise. All three organizations became enthusiastic Jam sponsors and their support would prove to be invaluable to the development of the Business Education Jam. Finally, in recognition of the tremendous reach of the Jam, the *Financial Times* joined as the global media sponsor of the Jam, providing research and outreach collaboration which would continue beyond the Jam. A full listing of Jam sponsors can be found in Appendix A.

With corporate and academic sponsors in place, content development began to accelerate. Through conversations with industry and academics the earliest framing of the Jam emerged in December 2013 as follows:

1. **Role of Business Schools**
   a. What should be the business models for business schools?
   b. To what degree should schools be partnering with firms?
   c. Are we providing adequate value for the cost?
2. **Research**
   a. What type of research is needed?
   b. What type of research will be most relevant?
3. **Experiential learning**
   a. What is the best way to close the gap between classroom and practice?
   b. How do we support entrepreneurship?
4. **Jobs**
   a. How will the skills needed for management change?
   b. What are the future jobs we are preparing students for?
   c. What are employers looking for? What will make employers hire our graduates?
   d. How do we organize career placement?
5. **Nature of graduate degree programs**
   a. Do we need specialists or generalists?
   b. What types of industry-specific knowledge need to be taught?
   c. Will there still be demand for the two-year MBA?
   d. If the MBA is dead what will replace it?
   e. Do we need shorter programs? Should they incorporate mandatory experiences?

6. **How do you judge the quality of business education?**
   a. Role of rankings
   b. Role of placements
   c. Role of cost
7. **What does it mean to be global?**
   a. What types of global experiences should schools offer?
8. **Executives – what do they need to retool?**
   a. Will there still be demand for an EMBA program?
   b. Will firms be willing to pay for an EMBA program?
9. **Role of industry in business education**
   a. How do we develop effective partnerships?
10. **Curriculum changes**
    a. Social enterprise – What should we be doing to incorporate social values?
    b. Ethics/values based leadership
       - How do we teach ethics?
       - How do we educate business students to be value based leaders?
       - How do we provide a sound ethical framework for making business decision?
       - Do we need external credentialing?

Each topic was of interest to the business education community yet there needed to be significantly more clarity in order to create effective forums for the Jam. To achieve this the Jam project team systematically engaged outside stakeholders to seek their counsel on themes they found relevant. Jam sponsors contributed feedback through frequent conversations, Deans and other academic leaders were consulted, and interested organizations such as the Business Higher Education Forum, PRME initiative, Association of MBAs, and New England Board of Higher Education were contacted. Deep industry perspective was also added through the engagement of the AACSB Business Practices Council, the corporate executive members of the Boston University Human Resources Policy Institute, and HR People + Strategy (SHRM's Executive Network) where an article on the Jam was published in the spring 2014 edition of the *People & Strategy* journal (Freeman, 2014). Each series of dialouge and engagement helped to deepen, enrich, and focus the potential

Jam themes. After the first seven weeks of content refinement the initial Jam themes emerged in February 2014 as follows:

Partners in Progress: Industry & Academia

Industry and academia are vitally important to each other, yet collaboration across the two is often limited. How can businesses, industry, and business schools forge more productive, reciprocal relationships? What is the role of recruiting, alumni, and curricular efforts in the relationship? Where are the areas in which partnerships could emerge? How will we know if partnerships are creating value?

Leading with integrity

Today's employers hire not only on experience but on ethics, character, and ability to lead with integrity. Which graduate characteristics are today's employers seeking? Can ethics and character be taught within a business school? Is the role of ethics changing? How do we cultivate teachable moments from practice? What is the role of organizational leaders in encouraging ethics?

Driving business research

The production of leading research is part of the mission of many business schools and informs industry in a rapidly changing world. But where is the best venue for research to occur? Is increased research conducted within the firm eroding academic research? How do business schools articulate the value of the research they produce? How should business research be supported, conducted, and disseminated? What is the benefit of research to society?

A new lifecycle of learning

There is no shortage of learning opportunities today – degrees, certificates, MOOCs, online, offline, and everything in between. Which learning opportunities are in demand? How do employers value or promote a lifecycle of learning? What specialized knowledge or skills are employees seeking? What is the role of business schools in supporting this lifecycle of learning and how can they do it better?

The innovation generation

Today's leaders break traditional educational paths as they create the innovation engines of tomorrow and are a key focus of today's hiring managers. How do students today learn differently? Is the role of academia being challenged? How do values impact the work environments they are seeking? How can employers manage and cultivate this new workforce? How do business schools remain relevant and create value?

Making an impact

Prospective students not only want to change their lives, they want to change the lives of others. How do business schools develop students for leadership in non-profit, social, and community settings? How do employers value this attribute? Do business schools need to rethink how they measure success and the impact of graduates?

In order to finalize content, the design of the Jam needed to be taken into consideration − particularly the size of the audience, to avoid too few forums with a high number of participants, or too many forums with a low number of participants. Each circumstance could reduce the effectiveness of the brainstorm. Also, each forum would require an expert host and VIP guests. There was difficulty in determining the final number of forums because of the outward facing design of the Jam which created difficulty in knowing a participant count in advance, unlike a corporate Jam with a defined pool of employees or stakeholders. Based on the feedback of IBM and the potential scope of participation a total of 10 forums would be created.

To enhance the final draft of the Jam content and provide a sense of whether it would resonate with Jam participants, IBM conducted a pre-listening study of social media. This study, which examined an exhaustive selection of social media use, took place from January 1 through May 31, 2014, and was designed to describe which topics were currently talked about, what was the typical sentiment for each topic based on social media mentions, and the potential level of engagement for each topic. To accomplish the study a list of keywords and phrases, based on the developed content, literature reviews, and examinations of social media, was created and provided to the IBM social analytics team. On June 24th the first pre-listening study was conducted and began to bring to life the breath of engagement on the potential topics:

	Total Mentions	Blogs	Forums	Twitter	News
Forum 1: Supporting 21st Century Competencies					
Workplace readiness	73	14	2	2	55
Workforce of the future	1,208	98	16	11	1,083
Global workforce	15,376	941	117	196	14,122
Skills gap	228	4	0	221	3
Skills gap	10,750	984	193	920	8,653
Skill gap	387	86	54	17	230
Skillsgap I skills gap I skill gap	11,263	1,058	242	1,127	8,836
Forum 2: Increasing the Value of Management Education					
Education ROI	7	0	0	1	6
MBA value	18	1	6	9	2
Alternatives to business school	3	0	0	3	0
Business school alternative	1	1	0	0	0
Specialized degree I specialized degrees	263	123	32	51	57
Specialized certificate(s)	183	22	3	0	158
Specialized degree I specialized degrees I specialized certificate I specialized certificates	446	145	35	51	215
Business education flexibility	0	0	0	0	0
Education flexibility	191	14	1	0	176
Individualized learning	462	67	2	1	392
Forum 3: Engaging New-Generation Students & Employees					
Millennials	39,718	5,738	1,224	8,616	24,140
Millennials in the workplace I millennials in workplace	148	34	8	54	52
Millennials in the workforce I millennials in workforce	448	12	0	2	434
Millennial education	2	0	0	1	1

(*Continued*)

	Total Mentions	Blogs	Forums	Twitter	News
Millennials and workplace	3,873	677	47	145	3,004
Millennials and workforce	5,332	713	85	114	4,420
Millennials and education	4,571	978	153	17	3,423
Forum 4: Cultivating Research Relevance & Rigor					
Business academic research	21	0	1	7	13
Research impact	385	46	4	11	324
Business research funding	6	1	0	2	3
Business research	42,682	4,496	1,087	7,361	29,738
Research funding	6,004	629	243	125	5,007
Academic research	16,137	1,731	1,090	151	13,165
Forum 5: Fostering Ethical Leadership					
Business ethics	39,103	5,829	2,883	21,674	8,717
Social responsibility	67,804	8,695	1,741	3,075	54,293
Teaching business ethics	234	20	1	58	155
Ethical decision making	478	238	27	80	133
Teaching ethics	91	32	2	17	40
Forum 6: Cultivating Innovation & Entrepreneurship					
Business education innovation	8	4	0	3	1
Business school curriculum reform	0	0	0	0	0
Entrepreneur ǀ entrepreneurship	788,016	86,552	18,639	413,023	269,802
Businessschoolincubat*	0	0	0	0	0
Bschoolincubat*	0	0	0	0	0
Incubation	16,451	2,061	1,365	2,129	10,896
Incubator(s)	63,692	7,257	2,208	14,652	39,575
Business curriculum reform	0	0	0	0	0

(*Continued*)

	Total Mentions	Blogs	Forums	Twitter	News
Curriculum reform	156	38	30	1	87
Forum 7: Driving Learning Experiences					
Pedagogy	3,894	1,662	246	107	1,879
Experiential learning	6,487	760	129	235	5,363
Outcome-based education	outcome-based education	89	40	21	2	26
Real-world	real world (excluding "business")	4,504	861	140	89	3,414
Forum 8: Harnessing Digital Technology					
Digital learning technology	digital learning technologies	66	5	0	0	61
Mooc(s)	massive open online course(s)	12,730	2,597	223	4,947	4,963
Online learning	online teaching	18,299	3,058	805	787	13,696
Online learning	16,882	2,604	723	618	12,937
Online teaching	1,826	535	83	169	1,039
Coursera	edx	udacity	khan academy	8,667	2,272	341	1,929	4,125
Online class	2,041	678	257	336	770
Online course	10,944	3,223	391	2,191	5,139
Forum 9: Challenging the Business Model of Education					
Education model	1,280	166	25	48	1,041
Funding	829,659	95,352	34,223	81,304	618,780
For-profit education	for profit education	1,441	169	23	38	1,211
Education funding	6,981	923	224	91	5,743
Forum 10: Advancing Policy & Governance					
Policy (excluding "business")	14,931	2,691	561	141	11,538
Accreditation	63,321	10,321	4,709	2,566	45,725
Governance	291,745	30,903	8,873	11,094	240,875

(*Continued*)

	Total Mentions	Blogs	Forums	Twitter	News
Rankings	177,194	41,252	7,568	10,757	117,617
Quality	2,565,979	493,241	222,606	198,221	1,651,911
Ranking I rankings	368,033	85,295	21,860	22,116	238,762
Governance & academia	2,314	463	50	3	1,798
Governance & business education	532	118	12	6	396
Governance & education policy	306	110	6	0	190
Quality & business education	5,275	730	98	32	4,415

IBM Social Insight Group, 2014.

This analysis quantified which topics were being discussed, who were the most cited sources, and what the relationships were across terms and themes. The first pre-listening highlighted terms which were not well cited or not as relevant to the conversation. The study keywords were refined and a final analysis of the top 18 concepts across social media related to the Jam was presented by IBM to the Jam team on July 27, 2014. This analysis helped to refine and validate the topics and on August 6, 2014 the final forum descriptions were created (see Appendix B).

3.4. Launching the Business Education Jam

In June 2014, attention began to focus on preparing the final elements of the Jam design and formally launching outreach to build registration interest. In alignment with other Jams, registration for the Business Education Jam would not be open until four weeks prior to the start of the event. However, given the external focus of the Jam it was recognized that significant outreach would have to occur in advance of the registration in order to achieve the desired participation goals.

The first effort in launching the Jam focused on building a robust website to serve as a "portal" for the Jam. Unlike the initial iteration of the Business Education Jam website, which was largely descriptive, a new dynamic and engaging site was prepared. The aim of this site was to proactively involve users on the Jam topics before the Jam even started. Essential literature related to the topic was highlighted, recent articles were showcased, and current research from partners including AACSB International, EFMD, PwC, and GMAC were all featured. To actively capture user interest a "pre-registration" form was also created so that users could be notified when registration began.

The second major effort focused on additional outreach to relevant organizations. In addition to formal sponsors, who had already planned to promote the Jam through their networks, other organizations were consulted and encouraged to participate so that their voice could be heard. Many, such as Principles for Responsible Management Education (PRME) and the Globally Responsible Leadership Initiative (GRLI), had expertise in specific areas of business education and were encouraged to engage with the Jam. Because registration and participation in the Jam was free and online it removed traditional barriers to participation.

The final effort to launch the Jam focused on social media. Although some selected print advertisements were used, a significant priority was placed on social media use to attract participants. The perceived benefits in using social media were the reduced cost, an ability to push out select Jam content to encourage feedback/engagement similar to that which occurs in the Jam, and the capability to track engagement across social media. A short animated video was released and became particularly helpful in explaining the concept of a Jam, which was unfamiliar to many. The most positive gains in social media were through LinkedIn and Twitter, as users of those platforms proved likely to engage in Jam content by sharing and commenting on it.

Coinciding with a formal press release on September 4, 2014, registration for the Business Education Jam opened and promotion through social media and online marketing increased. Registration began at a slow pace, with increasing numbers each week. The majority of registrations took place in the final week before the Jam as the excitement of the event began to spread more deeply across social media channels.

The Business Education Jam, while an online event, also had an incredible on-site presence. The "home base" of the Jam was the Executive Leadership Center of Boston University's Questrom School of Business. This space was fully transformed with Jam branding and fostered tremendous excitement for the event. The primary facilities for the Jam included: a dedicated room for media/on-demand use; a "command center" room, which included the IBM team, marketing/communications team, project leadership and VIPs; a dedicated room for Jam facilitators; and a large dining/casual space. Each space was open for the entire 60-hour duration of the Jam. The lobby of the Questrom School of Business was also transformed into an engaging "Jam Café" where anyone could stop by a series open laptops to register and participate.

The on-site activity of the Jam mirrored the design of the Jam itself: it was collaborative and engaging. Several VIP guests and hosts called the Jam command center home for their three days, including Dan LeClair, Executive Vice President & Chief Operation Officer of AACSB International; Howard Thomas, LKCSB Distinguished Term Professor of Strategic Management, Management Education Director, Academic Strategy and Consulting Unit, Singapore Management University; and Marie Wilson, Pro Vice Chancellor (Business and Law), University of South Australia Business School. Other VIP guests who stopped by the Jam command center at various points included Martin Nisenholtz, Former Chief Digital Officer, The *New York Times* Company; Robert A. Brown, President, Boston University; and Dr Johan Roos, Dean, CEO and Managing Director, Jönköping International Business School (JIBS). In addition to VIPs, members of industry including representatives from Santander Bank and Fidelity also participated in the Jam on-site.

During the Jam, social media use was particularly compelling. Just prior to the Jam, on September 29, there were a total of 3,601 users registered for the Jam. Once the Jam began social media use, in particular the @businessedjam twitter account, were leveraged to share Jam updates, discuss hot trends, and promote upcoming events. Participants also used social media to share their Jam experience and word began to spread quickly.

In the first day of the Jam an additional 1,049 users registered and by the completion of the Jam a total of 5,730 users had registered to take part in this global dialogue (IBM Jam Program Office, 2014). This incredible momentum in registration growth during the Jam itself was not only a testament to the interest in the event, but the Business Education Jam set the record for the highest percentage of in-Jam user registration growth of any previous IBM Jam event. For a full perspective on the breadth of users who engaged in the Jam, please see Appendix C. Following the completion of the Jam social media and the Business Education Jam website continued to be leveraged to share Jam findings and current news.

3.5. How the Business Education Jam Fostered a Brainstorm

The Business Education Jam was designed to become a platform for engaging stakeholders across the world. Although text based, the Jam was not a simple discussion board. Each element contributed to the broader goal of advancing conversation and creating ideas. The key features which helped to frame the Business Education Jam included:

- *Forums*: All jam content was structured into one of 10 forums. Each forum contained a title, key question, short description, and long description. Each focused on a key challenge facing business education and was framed to provide guidance for, but not to limit dialogue.
- *Jam hosts*: Each forum had one or two hosts who were respected leaders in their fields. To highlight the industry-academy collaborative nature of the Jam some forums included both an academic and industry host. The hosts each developed a remark in advance of the Jam which became the first post in the forum. From that point forward, hosts monitored their forums and helped to advance dialogue, link emerging ideas, and frame conversation. Hosts were provided analysis during the Jam and received guidance on how they could help to advance conversation.

An example of this was near the end of the Jam when each host posted a summary of themes and encouraged users to bring forward actions based off their many ideas.

- *VIP guests*: The 99 VIPs in the Jam provided excitement and expertise. Each was scheduled to enter the Jam during a defined hour so that users could look for them and potentially engage. This enabled the VIPs to contribute insightful comments and allowed any user to provide a response to the VIPs, which built additional user excitement. For a full listing of VIPs who engaged in the Jam see Appendix D.
- *Chat sessions*: A limited number of synchronous chat sessions were scheduled each day of the Jam to facilitate a deeper dive into topics. The chats were also led by VIP guests and provided the opportunity for users to engage with the VIPs on a more intimate scale. Most chats quickly filled to a capacity of no more than 25 users. Transcripts were made available to all Jam participants to inform conversation.
- *Facilitators*: On-site at the Jam headquarters in the Questrom School of Business were 10–20 facilitators engaging in the Jam at all times. Each facilitator played a role in advancing conversation by highlighting emerging trends, connecting threads with related topics, and prompting users to increase the clarity of their posts through targeted responses to advance dialogue.
- *Polls*: Throughout the Jam a number of short, multiple-choice polls were released to enable participants to quickly react to a specific question. Some polls were designed before the Jam based on the feedback of stakeholders during the content development process while others were created in response to trending topics. Polls were posted throughout the duration of the Jam and the results were made available to Jam participants and promoted through social media to prompt additional engagement.

All of these elements came together to help facilitate an energetic and informative global conversation. This alone, however, would not be enough to generate the ideas required to reimagine business education. That was the role of Jam participants who contributed more than 6,000 posts and represented 122 countries. Each participant brought with him or her unique perspectives, experiences, and ideas that collectively began to move the needle on thinking about business education. This open forum model of participation, or crowdsourcing of ideas, taking place on a digital platform that facilitates engagement brings with it significant potential. In January 2015 a summary of Jam findings was released in the report *Reimaging Business Education: A World of Ideas* and freely distributed at www.bu./jam (Reimaging Business Education, 2015). The Business Education Jam and the subsequent report were only the start of a global dialogue on the future of business education. How can features of open innovation further impact how we think about the future of business education? We begin to explore this question and others in Chapter 4.

4 The Emerging Impact of Open Innovation

The three days of the Business Education Jam saw researchers, scholars, students, executives, and thought leaders engaged in an unprecedented online brain-storming session about the future of business education. Conducted in collaboration with industry and academic collaborators and enabled by IBM technology, the Jam attracted over 5,000 participants from more than 40 industries, 350 academic institutions, and 122 countries.

Around the clock and around the globe these "Jammers" shared insights, experiences, and ideas about issues critical to business and business education including how to engage today's students and employees; imparting 21st century competencies; developing innovators for the future; fostering collaboration between industry and academia; and much more. Participants could join in from their laptop, desktop, or smartphone, begin a conversation, leave for a while, and come back without missing a beat, thanks to the full record and analysis the Jam technology provides.

What made the Business Education Jam unique is that it not only represented an opportunity to engage the broad set of actors affected by our current models of management education, but that the Jam itself was a deliberate case of open innovation.

The past dozen or so years have shown the great potential of open innovation and at the same time demonstrated the substantial changes required of existing organizations and markets when forces of openness begin to bear on them.

> Around the clock and around the globe "Jammers" shared insights, experiences, and ideas about issues critical to business and business education

To specify these changes and identify their potential impact on how we designed the Jam and the potential changes to business education itself, we will give a brief overview of open innovation.

4.1. Open Innovation

What do we mean by "open innovation"? The term was coined by Henry Chesbrough in 2003 (Chesbrough, 2003) based on his observation of how large organizations were enhancing their capacity for innovation by increasingly opening themselves up to their suppliers, partners, and customers. However, this process of "opening" to foster greater innovation has been around for centuries. The Longitude Prize in the 18th century is one great example (Dash, 2000) as it incentivized open participation in helping to solve a critical problem.

Openness did not become an approach which effected an entire industry or profession until the birth of free, or "open source," software in the late 1980s and early 1990s through the efforts of people such as Richard Stallman and Linus Torvald.

Bill Joy, the founder of Sun Microsystems, made the most famous statement regarding the impact that openness would have on the software industry when he said: "No matter who you are, most of the smartest people work for someone else" (Lakhani & Panetta, 2007). From his vantage point of working in the software industry in the early 1990s, he could see the significant changes that open source software would have on established software companies and how this approach would be a new way of "doing" innovation.

In 2005 Jeff Howe and Mark Robison (Whitla, 2009) coined the term "crowdsourcing" to describe the broad impact opening up was having across industries and how significant value could be created from distributed, rather than centralized, expertise.

InnoCentive was one of the early pioneers in creating value through crowdsourcing.

Launched by and spun out of Eli Lilly in 2003, the US-based firm eventually become a network of 500,000 users, who were referred to as "solvers," that addressed scientific and technical challenges. Challenges were posted on its website by both corporate and non-profit companies called "seekers." Successful solvers were paid for their work and their solutions transferred to seekers. InnoCentive's success in solving problems that had defeated other firms could range from 40% to 60% by opening up and "challenging" the crowd, thereby crowdsourcing the solution.

> The historic way of organizing innovation for the past 500 years has been to centralize it within the enterprise, whether it be a church, a university, or a corporation

Open innovation is now being applied to many different industries and challenges, including higher education. In fall 2015 the Raymond Mason School of Business at the College of William and Mary pursued changes to their MBA program through an open innovation effort called *Tomorrow's MBA: Co-Creating the Future of Business Education*. This online event solicited ideas and comments on the MBA design over seven weeks. Even broader, the Business Education Jam sought to apply the principles of open innovation to our profession and our industry.

There are three key characteristics of open innovation: people, problems, and process; and each was embodied in the design and execution of the Business Education Jam.

4.2. Characteristics of Open Innovation

4.2.1. PEOPLE

In keeping with Bill Joy's powerful insight it is important to identify who are the experts, where they are located, and who is participating when it comes to opening up for innovation.

Historically, the experts were individuals of high status and/or specialists in R&D, research centers, and academic departments. The historic way of organizing innovation for the past 500 years is to centralize it within the enterprise, whether it be a church, a university, or a corporation. This is done not only to control what is being created but also to make communication and testing easier.

Open innovation, on the other hand, increases both the volume of research and ideas and also the variety of people participating in the process.

One of the most powerful examples of a company opening itself up to a variety of people is the Chicago-based T-shirt retailer, Threadless.

Perhaps the most striking aspect of Threadless' open approach to innovation is that its community creates well over 800 new designs each week. Within a traditional "designer" company producing T-shirts, the number of alternative designs would be counted in single figures.

An exponential volume of designers could not create a final design in a silo and require the participation of a variety of others to provide feedback. For Threadless, fashion bloggers critique the designers, participants offer ideas, and the community engages in voting to narrow the final design selections. Why would these participants spend their time engaging in this process? Designers take part because they receive feedback on their designs for improvement, fashion and culture bloggers engage for exposure to new trends, and other community members with a general interest in design are offered unprecedented access to the process.

Size and variety are important considerations in open innovation as experiments fail when they do not attract enough participants with a wide enough variety of opinions to participate around issues they care about.

The recent failure of Quirky.com, a New York-based start-up with significant venture capital backing, is instructive because the company limited who could participate in designing, critiquing, and choosing what "products" Quirky would produce.

In a rather similar way, business schools have increasingly become much more like the universities that they are normally a part of – expertise is centered and siloed in academic departments. While academic departments may engage with alumni or recruiters, these forms of participation are often limited, and broader open dialogue on the future of a particular school or the business education industry is lacking. External stakeholders also have no avenues for engaging in the dialogue.

The Business Education Jam moved beyond the "ivory tower" and directly engaged all the key stakeholders in business education – students, faculty, administration, recruiters, alumni, accreditation boards, government, and business journalists – in order to develop critical insights to create a positive path forward.

4.2.2. PROBLEMS

The question of who participates and who are the experts naturally leads to the question of who chooses the focus of the problems and thus which are likely to be addressed. Equally, who participates and what problems they focus on is related to what these participants value.

The inherent value in open source software projects comes from the fact that participants choose the problems that are of the most interest to them, either because they are motivated to learn something new or because they live with a problem daily and strive to solve it in order to make progress in their learning or their work. As a result, there are no strong hierarchies or centralized experts telling participants what challenges to focus on. Rather, in open innovation problems are distributed – just like the people.

> Open innovation increases the volume and variety of participants and problems and therefore the potential dependencies that need to be identified, managed, or changed over time

In a more closed approach there may be only one type of expert participating, which likely leads to only one main problem to address. In business education, the problems that are focused on are narrowly defined by strong disciplinary dynamics (academic departments) and hierarchical structures (administration, accreditation bodies) resulting in an approach that is much more closed than open.

The Business Education Jam needed to attract all stakeholders and recognize that each would bring different problems they desired to solve. In business education the faculty determine the primary problem to focus on; that is, teaching and grading. However, while students may want a good grade, the primary problem that they want to solve is getting a job they really want. Alumni, on the other hand, want to stay connected to their school and remain up to date with their skills. Often, though, that relationship from the university's or schools' point of view is defined by development and fundraising activities. Recruiters want job candidates with the right set of skills while schools are focused on successful placement, not successful skillsets. It is not surprising that there are so many disconnects among all the stakeholders who participate in business education.

What the Jam enabled was connection of those various participants and generation of conversations that allowed them to not only identify their respective problems, but also collaborate across the community to develop solutions.

4.2.3. PROCESSES AND TOOLS

Open innovation increases the volume and variety of participants and problems and therefore the potential dependencies that need to be identified, managed, or changed over time.

This increases the complexity and requires a greater capacity to coordinate and take collective actions that generate distributed consequences. There are more degrees of freedom about design or who participates, what they will focus on doing, and who will evaluate outcomes and the value that will be produced.

Perhaps the greatest potential of open innovation stems from the increasing complexity and dependencies of the who, what, and how (evaluation) of the process. This results in promoting a great capacity for experimentation and validation of value, both in how existing value is captured and how new value is created (innovation).

Processes and tools are shared methods for specifying the dependencies across actions and evaluating the distributed outcomes across all those dependencies. This produces learning that produces more actions. Processes generate signals of evaluation and value to a distributed set of actors potentially focused on different problems that allow for collective action.

In the open source software business shared tools including compilers for testing code and version control systems, allow the coordination of action and the collective assessment of interdependent work.

In the Business Education Jam the 10 forums related to particular challenges and different stakeholders' interests got the conversations started and are also related to the critical questions posed in Chapter 2. Facilitators participated in the conversation helping to support it and also making connections to related threads of conversation. The 10 forums helped to establish initial dependencies that evolved as the conversations finished, new themes emerged, and new conversations with new people took place.

4.3. Open Innovation Increases the Capacity for Experimentation

The power of open innovation is that it not only organizes distributed expertise but also more importantly, it creates dependencies and coordinates experimentation across more people and their problems. This leads to an increase in learning and collective deliberate actions, thus swelling meaningful activities in the core engine of innovation.

For open source software the capacity to connect and then assess the consequences of distributed efforts is accomplished through key technologies such as modular code/kernel, shared testing compilers, and version control systems. This is what allows distribution expertise and experimentation to work together to generate a greater capacity for innovation.

Organizing for distributed innovation has proved much harder in non-software environments where shared testing methods do not exist or are not as precise as they are in software development

The Jam is an initial attempt to generate participation from all stakeholders to identify common themes and challenges that can be further addressed with additional open innovation efforts.

4.4. The Challenge for Business and Higher Education Is a Collective Problem

As we think about the long-term benefits of pursuing an open innovation approach to business education which extends beyond the Jam, we must recognize that we can easily underestimate the challenges since they go beyond the level of a school or university, to a broad-based collective and professional level.

The biggest problems lie at the professional level and this makes it very hard for well-established universities to break out into new approaches. Existing institutions in higher education – business schools, in particular – seem almost powerless to change despite significant hand-wringing due to changing graduate enrollments and dramatic shifts in the education landscape.

This collective challenge also makes it very hard for new approaches to business education to adequately scope the tasks that need to be integrated and so they end up problematically fragmented or narrow. The early optimism about new approaches such as MOOCs as a universal solution, for example, has faded as learning solutions require integration across more skills and sets of problems.

What level of substantial change must be anticipated for us to pursue the benefits of open innovation beyond the Jam itself?

To scale the potential changes in business education it is instructive to look again at the software industry and its evolution as more "open" approaches have taken hold. This evolution can then be a guide as we consider "how" participation across business education's widely differing stakeholders can be organized.

In the 1980s and 1990s the dominant software industry model was the creation of "products," very often in the form of boxed software created by experts in centralized R&D teams.

These products were licensed to customers and sold as upgrades or a new version (i.e., 1.0; 2.0, etc.) with new features.

This industry model changed in the early 2000s as the concept of software as a service began to take hold. Software was now produced to meet the more specific needs of the actual end-user rather than bundled sets of features determined by centralized experts. Software began to be seen as an "on demand" service and as a result features became more customized and tailored to establishing value on an ongoing basis.

Subsequently, this service orientation drove the software industry to embark on a broader and bolder move which connected developers and users directly to provide the almost continuous creation and exchange of innovations. This final step toward a "platform" orientation allows for the principles of open innovation first pioneered in open source software to be realized in the broader software industry.

Thus software was born as a platform, which can be most dramatically seen in such companies as SalesForce.com and their creation of Force.com as an innovation platform.

We anticipate that business education will evolve along a similar path, not just offering products/courses developed by specialists but becoming a service which is consumed by students and others to meet their current needs. Business education can evolve to become a platform that will facilitate interaction across all stakeholders as they share expertise, problems, and solutions which generate relevant and timely knowledge and skills for all participants.

Products or services do not vanish when a platform approach to innovation and competition is taken. Rather, a platform approach makes those products or services more innovative and useful, which in turn allows for further experimentation.

Indeed, the Business Education Jam is itself a platform approach. It connected a global population while addressing a large set of problems through collective conversation. As a result, sharable challenges were identified which can be addressed with follow-on efforts by those with the courage and foresight who are motivated to address those challenges for a better future.

We see the Jam as a ground breaking, initial, and essential step in the evolution of business education.

5 Addressing the Gap between Theory and Practice

A range of media outlets have ensured there has been no shortage of criticism on the state of business education in recent years. Such criticisms include everything from it being too expensive, indulging in teaching methods that are old fashioned, being captives of rankings that drive too much but tell us too little, questioning of the relevancy of management research, and a tenure system that shores up the ivory towers.

Consequently we know we need to change and innovate but what should we as an "industry" – as schools, faculty, students, and employers – do to advance a compelling agenda?

The purpose of the Business Education Jam was to begin to move beyond criticism to establish constructive dialogue, define choices, and ultimately foster purposeful action. The reality is that the choices and actions of various stakeholders in business education will be seen from different vantage points. Our challenge was to develop a framework that makes sense of what was learned from the Jam and to establish coherent action for all involved.

The Business Education Jam was initially viewed as a conference with a "twist": "Although the structure is similar to a conference, in which the schedule is planned around specific forums and themes, participants will be exposed to different socially driven tools meant to prompt conversation, from polls and word clouds to chats with featured guests" (Landry, 2014).

The Jam framework identifies the current challenges faced by various stakeholders and goes further to unearth the underlying structure of our industry that produced these challenges in the first place. This understanding then informs and guides stakeholder actions.

As the design – and breadth – of the Jam continued to develop, the potential power of the frameworks established became increasingly clear:

> Applause to the Business Education Jam, the big online collaboration that launches tomorrow, for seeking to better understand and address the "supply and demand gap" between the needs of employers and the output of business schools. This type of conversation – between business schools and industry – is critical as business schools around the globe seek objective guideposts as they reimagine their business models so as to retain their relevance in an environment turned on its head by a storm of disruption. Companies, too, have a lot at stake in this conversation. (Westerbeck, 2014)

As a Jam participant clearly stated: "Part of what this Jam is attempting to accomplish is how we bridge academia with industry" – the so-called THEORY-PRACTICE "relevance" gap.

> In many ways prototypes in architecture and the patient in medicine allows for a middle ground between theory and practice. Having this middle ground where theory is readily applied has allowed these professional schools to avoid many of the criticisms that business education faces today

5.1. The THEORY-PRACTICE Gap

The overriding feature of this framework is that it must describe the fundamental gaps that have been mentioned by many, both as criticisms and also as challenges for the future.

These gaps are expressed in terms of:

- teaching versus research
- applied versus theoretical
- experiential versus existing pedagogy
- real world versus narrow theory

The theory-practice gap exists across many professional domains (Nuthall, 2004; Trahan & Gitman, 1995; Upton, 1999) and is particularly acute in professional schools including architecture, medicine, and business that have clear academic values but serve changing professional communities with strong ties to dynamic job markets. Professional schools manage this gap with varying degrees of success.

Architecture has been successful in managing the theory-practice gap as its medium of communication is largely via physical objects – drawings or scale models, for example – that can be shared across experts (faculty) and novices (students). This sharing often takes place in a studio setting where concepts, prototypes, presentations, comments, and criticisms are deeply embedded in an iterative design approach.

The advent of digital-based design tools has enhanced the ability to drive collaboration and problem solving across the different disciplines involved in turning a design into a reality (Boland, Lyytinen, & Yoo, 2007). Thus, what starts as a concept in one domain is made applicable to concepts in other domains and each are then refined and improved collectively.

Medical education has addressed the gap through its clinical approaches to training in hospital settings along with the "teaching" role that goes on between novices and experts. Thus, theory taught from a given discipline is applied around an actual patient or in a laboratory setting. This allows for the appreciation of different disciplines and, more importantly, how they are applied to the complexity of the human body to create a diagnosis and/or a solution.

One Jam participant specifically highlighted this dynamic: "In the medical school model, medical schools align with teaching hospitals, which support the teaching of practical skills through clinical encounters. Similarly, business schools could partner with "teaching companies," which support the teaching of practical skills by entrenching business students in day-to-day operations in a particular company/organization.

These partnerships could benefit all three parties in the long run (school, business/organization, and student)!"

In many ways prototypes in architecture and the patient in medicine allows for a middle ground between theory and practice. This has enabled these professional schools to avoid many of the criticisms that business schools face today in terms of the disconnect of how and what they teach and the relevance of the research they produce (Christensen & Carlile, 2009).

Overarching prototypes are difficult, if not impossible, to find in business education. True, the case study has been relatively successful in providing a prototype-like setting where theory and practice can be combined in meaningful ways. Students apply concepts they are being taught to a practical context and develop a more sophisticated understanding of what the concepts mean and a greater ability to use them in future settings.

The challenge for business education is that we do not have prototypes of the same veracity and scalability as in architecture or medicine. In fact, one can argue that a key challenge of business education is that it is so "siloed" by different disciplines that students face a multitude of competing and incommensurate methods and prototypes. This is why the complexity of business renders it the most challenging context in which to manage the theory-practice gap.

The irony of the situation is that in 1959, as the Ford Foundation and Carnegie Foundation reports testify, business education was regarded as *too much* on the side of practice: as not conceptually rigorous; as having no theory and scientific measure to guide it; and hence susceptible to fads or poor ideas.

The reaction to these two pivotal reports over 50 years ago unwittingly began the expansion of a gap that must now be addressed.

The figure below represents this gap between theory and practice; a gap that the case study method and internships have been unsuccessful in narrowing. Indeed, the deep tension that now exists between theory and practice must be urgently tackled.

The Theory-Practice Gap

Practice ◄━━━━━━━━━━━━━━━━━━━━━► Theory

5.2. The Tension of Specialization and Integration

This movement toward theory and conceptual rigor significantly increased the tension between the specialization of knowledge and the integration of knowledge that is a part of any theory-practice gap. Academic disciplines such as economics, sociology, psychology, and mathematics that began coming into business education in the 1960s and 1970s brought science-based methodologies and conceptual typologies to the study of the "functional" areas of business and management, which created siloed specializations that we see today.

Management teachers moved from being "functional" specialists with a generalist orientation (focused on a given "functional" practice) to specialists with exclusively a disciplinary orientation.

Further, since "published" research is the currency of the realm and proof of scientific rigor, faculty became specialized around academic disciplines and the peer-reviewed journals that legitimized that currency. Over time the focus and allegiance of teaching moved from that of "functional skill" in a given business discipline to disciplinary knowledge shared and evaluated by a small community of scholars.

Therefore the frameworks faculty used became increasingly specialized; the problems they focused on became increasingly specialized; and the means by which they evaluated those problems and created value became increasingly specialized.

The figure below reveals that not only has the gap between theory and practice opened up, it has been made even more severe due to the dramatic tension produced by the specialization of knowledge in relation to its integration.

Thus, significant questions loom including: Who are the integrators?; What are the important problems around which integration can take place?; and What processes are in place to facilitate a pedagogical integration across siloed knowledge, faculty, and courses in the future?

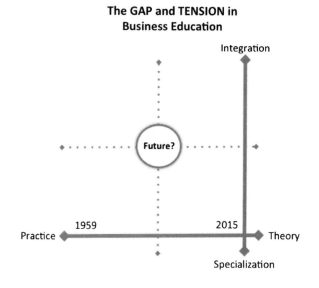

5.3. The Cycle Time of Experimentation and Learning

The key outcome of open innovation is the increased capacity for experimentation and learning involving many different people and their problems. The challenge of open innovation is orchestrating the interactions of an increasingly wide-ranging group of people, their problems, and their means of valuing their solutions.

When you put this challenge up against the gap and tension now present in business education it is apparent that our capacity for pedagogical experimentation and learning is significantly hampered. Business education often is a knowledge-transfer approach to learning where experts lecture to students and then assess their retention of that knowledge through testing.

The more than 70 years old case study method is an improvement over lectures. Although the case study method has its strengths, it is increasingly regarded as a dated means of applying knowledge in a classroom setting. The fact that there is one business school in the world that drives the vast majority of case development is evidence of a centralized rather than an open approach to experimentation, variety and learning. The case method as the dominant state of the art is a reminder that important changes in business education are long over due. Business schools need to be concerned about the state of case study pedagogy and focus on better addressing the practical and experiential aspects of business school education.

> Not only has the gap between theory and practice opened up it has also been made even more severe due to the dramatic tension produced by the specialization of knowledge in relation to its integration

> Once we see the underlying topography that arose between 1959 and 2015 we can easily see why we are so constrained by it

One Jam participant, an academic with over 20 years' experience in business schools, said: "One of the major concerns in development of skills that will be necessary for the 21st century is the ability to deal with ambiguity. With a traditional case, especially when based on actual events, the task is to generate the right answer – which is the opposite of working with ambiguity."

To help resolve this, the participant recommended moving toward a "live" case method: "In my undergraduate organizational communication classes, student teams are each given a company, preferably a non-US company, facing some kind of current issue. The students are given questions but their findings are evaluated in terms of how well they have organized the process. Because there are no pre-determined right answers, the students have to work within a more open framework."

When we look at medical education the clinical approach has been a very successful means of maintaining a balance between theory and practice. That method is focused on a particular patient who is of consequence to the faculty and students at the school. The patient – the focus of the clinical approach – is examined by different specialists to solve his or her problem. However, in business schools the focus of a case study is usually developed and delivered by a specialist with limited opportunities for integration of thought across disciplines.

> When we examine business education it has become an increasingly closed system, despite its professed connection to the practice of business and its obligation as a professional school for the effective training of business students.

Once we see the underlying topography that arose between 1959 and 2015 we can easily see why we are so constrained by it. In fact, one can easily argue that it has become a system that limits who is involved, whose problems are addressed, and what value is being created.

A higher education leader commented during the Jam, when considering how to effectively build student skills, that, "I would go a step further and work with business and major corporations to help mold the actual business schools and their teaching and delivery methods. Apple, Samsung, Google, IBM, or any number of major companies, should be partnered with to further the deep integration of business skills and knowledge within the business schools. If we want our students to work in the real world, then we need them to get this real-world experience in our own educational programs of study. This isn't just through case studies and theory, this is through partnerships with real-world businesses that help us build what we need."

The lack of success in providing an educational platform to drive appropriate learning and practice-based experiences is almost tragic, especially when it is apparent that other professional schools have managed this gap and tension with some success. Business education must now attempt to answer such urgent questions as: How do students participate in learning; How do employers shape what is being learned and participate in it; What is the role of faculty; and Who is driving the interactions across all these participants?

5.4. Looking for a Guide: From Products to Services to Platforms

We have identified the underlying forces and landscape that have created the tensions and disconnects in business education. Can we now determine whether there is a reliable guide forward among the myriad of critiques and suggestions that emerged from the Jam?

In the Jam many of these critiques and suggestions focused on traditional program elements. For example, comments related to faculty ranged from questioning tenure: "because the specialized tenure track and its publishing requirements is [forcing] the trend toward greater specialization in academia ... in the opposite direction from industry [which] is asking for new insights that can be deployed/integrated in complex business settings," to a broader re-envisioning of the backgrounds of faculty: "I think teaching as a second or third career will make older, more experienced professors an increasingly important part of the mix. We bring experience and education — and we love sharing our skills with others or we wouldn't still be working!"

Comments on courses included dialog on how we approach course design: "Why not approach curriculum/course development like good product development — engage the final customers (employers) up front to get their priorities and then [have] faculty design the course [product] using that employer input, combined with other design inputs?" to specific pedagogy, such as the value of experiential education: "Are we trade schools or higher-education institutions? If we want experiential learning, then why not just go to work? Experiential learning has a lot of variables to help predict and measure the desired learning outcome."

Others took the conversation to another level, envisioning a landscape fully changed, bringing in design thinking, partners, and co-generated experiences. As one Jam participant noted:

> I'm part of a small team at a top London design school planning a new kind of MBA centered on innovation and leadership, rooted in a design school pedagogy. We've been learning along the way from MOOCs, open platforms, and events such as OpenIDEO and hackathons, as well as experiments in degree programs.
>
> We think the future of management education is much more closely tied to doing and action learning rather than being taught. It's somewhere closer to change

networks, and peer-to-peer learning and flipped classrooms, not reliant on faculty, who are often more interested in research, and on partnerships with relevant organizations that want to hire the people who emerge and engage with the learning along the way.

Central to this learning approach is problem-based learning by doing, which develops students as reflective practitioners (Donald Schon). This approach supports them into taking action and having expertise in context and helps them reflect on what they are doing. In the new MBA program we are creating at Central Saint Martins, we are trying to combine this pedagogy with a conventional MBA curricula – and we are conceiving of what we are doing as a prototype and the students and our partners as co-designers and co-users with us.

Not surprisingly, the principles of openness are themselves a help and have been at work in other industries so it is important to see how those industries have evolved from a more closed approach to learning, innovation, and change.

As suggested at the end of Chapter 4 the software industry is a meaningful guide and metaphor for the process of evolution from closed to more open approaches to learning and innovation. Further, it demonstrates the strategic challenges that existing organizations face as they attempt to "shift" their focus and evolve.

For most of their history software companies focused on creating products – boxed software – as they competed and made money. This product-based approach is not surprising since this is how most companies have focused their innovative efforts and strategies across nearly all industries. Even the catch-all notion of disruption originated as a case of a cheaper product being developed and causing the disruption.

The software industry showed us the first widespread evolution to a new way of innovating and competing through the shift from a product focus to a service focus in the early 2000s.

Primarily driven by the interconnectivity of the internet, this change lowered the costs of serving end-users. Consequently, a product approach to innovation began to make way for an on-demand approach; products now became on-going services that individuals and companies could consume like a utility.

This resulted in a dramatic shift: the goal was no longer to create a product with a massive feature set and then resell and license it to customers through the next version, but rather to connect more closely with what end-users are actually "doing" and help address the problems they have yet to solve. This re-directs and distributes the location of the innovation.

Although not the first to pursue this service-based approach, SalesForce is the most dramatic example because its founder came out of the enterprise software world (Oracle, SAP, IBM) that was famous for very expensive, bulky, and expansive software as a product. SalesForce founder Eric Benioff came from Oracle and saw a service-based approach as a way to more openly interact with the end-user and create value in a new way. This approach eventually was labeled SaaS (software as a service) and has changed the nature of competition in the software industry.

There would be a further evolution of more open approaches to innovation and competition that started almost unnoticed in the early 1990s in the open source software movement. Although code had been open before, Linus Torvalds initiated a more dramatic approach when in August 1991 he posted a UNIX programming problem to a USENET user board asking what they would like to see in their code (Torvalds, 1991). By the end of that year the LINUX kernel was released and the potential of connecting programmers with a problem and for programmers to interact – and hence the power of Linux as an open innovation model – was born.

There have been many other successful OSS projects, including Apache and Firefox. What unites each of them is that they operate as a connected service over the internet with shared tools (code compilers, version control systems, etc.). This has enabled them to interact, collaboratively work and solve each other's problems, and increased the capability to experiment, learn, and overall innovate beyond what was previously possible. The focus on innovation became creating a means for people with problems and solutions to interact in ways to solve those problems.

> The software industry showed us the first widespread evolution to another way of innovating and another way of competing; and that began with the shift from a product focus to a service focus in the early 2000s

> If we use the pattern of evolution in software as a guide, we now see that many industries are changing not just because of interconnectedness of new technologies but the potential that openness provides for innovation and value creation

The evolution of the innovative potential of software extended from the model of a product, created by centralized experts, to an on-demand service. And, ultimately to a platform that provides the means for people to interact to share problems, develop solutions, and create value more rapidly.

In 2007 SalesForce launched Force.com as a true platform (PaaS; Platform as a Service) to allow those with potential solutions to interact with those looking for a solution. For SalesForce, Force.com became the primary engine of R&D that matched the localized and rapid demands that a service-based approach created. The traditional R&D approaches of a product strategy became too slow, too bloated, and too expensive. It is hard to ignore the struggles that Oracle and SAP have experienced as they move from their centralized R&D approach to a very different open platform approach to innovation.

If we use the pattern of evolution in software as a guide, we see that many industries are changing because of the interconnectedness of new technologies and the potential that openness provides for innovation and value creation. We see this with GE's industrial internet approach as a way to think beyond its massive installed base of products toward deep partnerships and open technology platforms (Iansiti & Lakhani, 2014). This is also seen in the non-profit approach to drug discovery with the Myelin Repair Foundation (Lakhani & Carlile, 2010) and in government with NASA's heavy use of open innovation platforms to extend the reach of innovation (King & Lakhani, 2013).

Each of these efforts focuses on creating services that support the development of platforms for interaction and innovation. Products are still offered but the emphasis and locus of innovation and experimentation is facilitated by a platform approach. When we think about how an industry, and individual organizations in an industry, respond to forces of change and greater openness this layered model represents transitions that must be managed for the evolution to occur (also see Iansiti and Lakhani, 2014 for a similar framework).

Evolution of an Industry (Software):
What about Business Education?

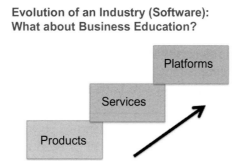

5.5. Driving Evolution in Business Education

This leads us to how we will think about the evolution of the current state of business education.

Unfortunately, business schools are dominated by a product approach which orients what they focus on and value. Examine most business schools and you will find they make strategic choices about two primary products: courses and publications. Students and programs are a distant third.

On the teaching side, courses are closest to what student's value and, on the research side, publications are closest to what research faculty value. In respect to teaching, business schools offer a variety of programs but the specific courses taught, how they are staffed, when they are updated, the identification of core content and electives are usually determined by faculty with limited direct input from students or employers. Hence, just like enterprise software and it centralized R&D approach this is an extremely closed approach. Some advanced electives in the senior year of undergraduate programs or the second year of the MBA can be focused on consulting projects with companies but represent a small number of the courses that students take. This course based focus often overlooks the integrated and dynamic needs of business education programs.

How does business education evolve to create more value?

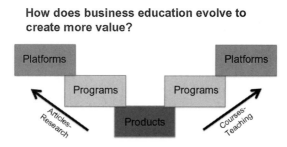

To deliberately move through this evolution to a service approach we must focus not just on the students but also on the purpose and rationale of the programs. What skills and perspectives, for example, do employers and alumni want?

Thus, just like moving from software as a product to a service, the question of whose educational needs are being met and whose problems are being solved (specialist faculty or employers who have changing needs or students who need up-to-date skills and perspectives) needs to be critically examined.

Developing academic programs as a service innovation requires opening things up and decentering the role (and control) of faculty as the primary experts in determining course design and content. The challenge then faced when developing a service-based approach is the need for increased awareness of the problems of students (i.e., the learning styles of millennials; what assessment approaches help drive experimentation and application) and the problems of companies (i.e., what skills are recruiters demanding? what perspectives are unique to different industries?). The obvious need is to develop a solution (the design of a program) that connects the problems of students and employers to generate solutions for both.

A clear challenge that arises with a service approach and better identification of the evolving needs of various users is to keep today's needs in plain view, understand and anticipate how needs are and will change, and develop solutions to address those changes. This calls for even greater openness and an ongoing need to ask those participating to identify, update, and address the resulting skills gaps.

As in the software example, the only way to stay up to date is to open up debate about what problems should be focused on and what are the sensible solutions for the various stakeholders in the platform (in this case students and potential employers). How can this approach become an essential design element for organizing a program (the service layer)?

We address this question by exploring and examining the service and platform design of the new Master of Science in Management Studies (MSMS) program in the Boston University Questrom School of Business.

5.6. Extending the Boundaries of Business Education: The Questrom School of Business MSMS Program and Partnered-Based Learning

Master of Science in Management Studies (MSMS) and Master of Science in Management (MSM) are recent additions to business school offerings. There are currently over a dozen programs in the United States and many more in European business schools.

In 2014, the Questrom School of Business evaluated those programs to see if we wanted to add an MSMS to our portfolio of graduate programs. Our examination revealed that virtually all of these programs were essentially a watered down MBA. A school will offer its traditional MBA "core" curriculum in a one-year format to a young graduate audience (generally with no work experience and typically very international), focusing on upskilling students for the entry-level job market.

This move by most schools is a self-confessed effort to increase graduate enrollment and revenues and does not represent an "innovation" approach to education. After examining these programs and the results of the Jam, we were motivated to develop a radical approach for our MSMS program at Questrom. We would take an open innovation approach to help us address the gap and tension in business education.

Developing programs as a service innovation is fundamentally about opening things up and decentering the role (and control) of faculty as the primary experts in determining course design and content

This approach to learning was more than just experiential or project based. It was what we now call "partner-based learning" across all of our teaching modules

The Pedagogical Solution to the GAP in Business Education

Most conversations about graduate programs start with: "How do we increase enrollments?" In our case, we started with identifying a problem that potential students faced in terms of what business skills and perspectives they were missing. Instead of targeting a general audience we focused on undergraduate students who have received their degrees without significant business oriented work experiences, from the STEM (science, technology, engineering, mathematics) fields or otherwise had strong analytic training. We found a set of students who, while they enjoyed their STEM oriented undergraduate programs, were looking for something more applied; closer to where science and technology were being applied; and something closer to business.

Recruiters and employers were also engaged, again in a targeted fashion to companies focused on science, technology, innovation and the importance of analytic skills. What we found after talking to both sides is that each was missing a bridge connecting themselves to the other; students taking their science and analytic skills and applying them in a business world context and companies finding students with science and analytics backgrounds with strong business skills. There are very few ways for undergraduates to get from STEM to business and, for companies, few STEM undergraduates have the skills to business the way an undergraduate in business would. What we have also heard from companies is that business undergraduates do not have "a passion for science" or a "strong analytical mindset" that they are looking for.

We fashioned the MSMS program to be a platform that links these two groups in a dynamic fashion. To do this we had to decenter the role of faculty as experts and question the dominant role that "courses" play in how we design learning. We felt strongly that the way to build an applied setting, with real-world assessment and high personal motivation, would be to focus throughout the program on "live" challenges faced in companies. This is a principle of openness, designing "challenges" or problems to yield value to a variety of participants and as a result encouraging interaction.

This approach to learning was more than just experiential or project based; it was what we now call "partner-based learning" across all of our teaching modules.

The primary goal of Module 1 is to expose the MSMS students to all of the functional languages of business (accounting, finance, marketing, operations, organization behavior) and apply these new languages to solving the unique challenges faced by a small retail organization.

In Module 2 the goal is to teach students the use of qualitative and quantitative data and how it can be used to help a large science and data company grow a part of its business.

The focus of Module 3 is to teach students organizational change, innovation, and strategy as they help a global technology firm become more nimble in response to significant changes that now require it to be more customer facing.

The modules evolve from less complex to more complex skills, and from small to very large business contexts.

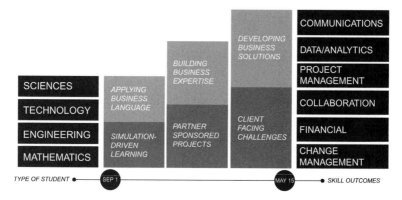

We choose partners with whom we have multiple relationships: sector/industry alignment, recruiting, alumni, and challenges of common interest. We also partner directly with our career center staff as they develop tailored approaches to help each student achieve their professional ambitions.

As an example of partner-based learning in Module 2, we partnered with Quintiles around a challenge they were facing. Quintiles executives provided training around specific issues associated with the challenge and mentoring to the student teams as they developed their solutions. Accenture also provided training in project management as well as additional mentoring.

The students work with four faculty who collectively cover the primary business disciplines as a cohesive team. The faculty role, given the challenge focus, is primarily as a facilitator and coach rather than as lecturer. Additional faculty are brought in on demand to cover skills and perspectives necessary to address the emergent nature of live challenges.

Our guiding principle is that we design our pedagogy around "real" challenges sponsored by our partners. This is why there is very little focus on courses or any traditional pedagogical approach or a traditional syllabus. To do so would not make room for placing the challenges at the center of the program and then meeting demand needs during the process.

This is the essence of the MSMS approach; partner-based learning that requires all involved to be united in creating value for all constituents, who each interact constantly through this platform approach to education.

What actually happens in the program? The challenge creates the pace, shapes the content, and motivates student learning. As a rule of thumb, the faculty can plan 70% of the content in advance. The remaining 30% emerges as all partners (faculty, company sponsors, students) work to drive the learning process.

Further, the classroom environment is meant to mirror a work setting where the task and challenge shapes the work and the content. Students meet in a dedicated classroom and work from 9am to 4pm for four days a week. Nearly all student work is team based and feedback is provided individually to students from the faculty team as well as from 360 degree feedback from team members. Reviews focus on outlining personal strengths and weaknesses and inviting students to engage in deep self-reflection. There are no tests, rather assessments are made to confirm the acquisition of specific skills. Addressing the challenges is the means by which the integration of skills and perspectives are demonstrated.

> As a rule of thumb, the faculty can plan 70% of the content in advance but the remaining 30% emerges as all partners work to drive the learning process as students engage in understanding and addressing the challenge

Grades are assigned as high pass, pass, or fail, similar to how feedback is given in the working world. Overall the MSMS program focuses on a "work" orientation to business challenges. We focus on skills and not courses, learning from failing fast and often and not through testing and drilling down, as well as a requirement to integrate across business disciplines to develop the most useful solution.

The challenge of embracing all that we know about experiential learning, live cases, and flipped classrooms is that one must step away from courses as the primary product of education and instead think about learning as a service delivery around "challenges." With that shift of focus you can then construct a platform where partners can interact, deliver value, and create value for each other. Perhaps ironically, this includes the students who must not be allowed to be trapped as passive, lecture-hearing, test-taking, and comment-making performers. Instead, they must become fully engaged experimenters who can also create value for faculty and the companies involved.

In summary, the principles of open innovation help us see the evolution from products, to services to platform that is transforming industries around the world. These principles also help us address who needs to participate, whose problems become central, and the integration and facilitation processes that will yield results in the context of business education.

5.7. What about Research, the Other Product of Academics?

About 70% of the comments during the Jam focused on teaching and pedagogy. The rest focused on research and, in particular, how to make it more relevant to business.

> The challenge of embracing all that we know about experiential learning, live cases, and flipped classrooms is that one must step away from courses as the primary product of education and instead think about learning as a service delivery around "challenges."

One Jam comment was: "The whole area of relevance to practitioners is often ignored. We need research to include more relevant dependent variables like profit, sales, pricing, valuation ratios, and so on. I believe industry needs much more help from academics but it is very difficult for many academics to be easily understood."

Others questioned who the audience for research should be: "While the emphasis on publication in research journals continues to dominate reward and recognition, the impact of research on the corporate world will continue to be limited. If we can see research output as a range of options – articles of general interest, tweets, teaching cases for classroom discussion, and so on, in addition to journal publication – then we can broaden the readership and engagement with multiple audiences, including corporate practitioners."

Still others also questioned the research impact in the classroom: "Faculty are often guided by their own inner light and protected by tenure to go in a direction that may not add much value. I have attended discussion sessions at professional meetings whose topic was 'how we can't let practice influence the classroom.' I get that researchers need the freedom to develop new means, modes and methods, but the majority of management scholars are not doing this type of research."

If the MSMS program is one experiment to rebalance the current state of the theory-practice gap and its over-emphasis on specialization, what experiments might we run on the research side given the constraint symbolized by specialized academic journals?

For example, in the field of medicine we have seen the experiment of translational medicine take hold over the last several years. The impetus behind translational medicine stems from the desire to get the sheer volume of specialized scientific knowledge "from the bench to the bedside" more rapidly.

Translational medicine is an attempt to manage the tension that increasingly specialized academic research adds to the theory-practice gap and establishes collaborations and standards that make it easier to integrate scientific knowledge across scientific disciplines and across the different stages of developing medical treatments.

What could be our equivalent of translational medicine in management education? Who would be involved? What problems would we focus on? Could it evolve in the same way as the pedagogical side of business education as it moves from products, to services, to platforms? How do principles of openness offer an evolutionary guide to create more interactions across more participants and ultimately more value for the societies that a professional school strives to serve? It is questions such as these which begin to prompt us to begin to reimagine business education.

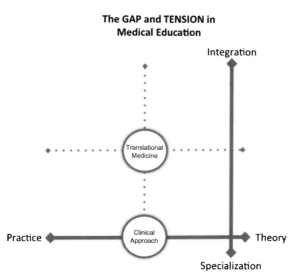

The GAP and TENSION in
Medical Education

CHAPTER

6

Reimagining Business Education

O ur premise has all along been that business education and the institutions engaged in the design, development, and delivery of business education are at an inflection point – and one that is very different from 1959. As we discussed in Chapters 2, 4, and 5, the pendulum has swung from being overly focused on practice in the 1950s to being overly guided by theory and research within specialized silos in the early 21st century.

The discussions and debates that motivated the Business Education Jam, the thrust of conversations during it, and the focus of presentations summarizing the key points from the Jam have all centered on highlighting two fundamental orthodoxies within business schools today: our approaches to (1) teaching and pedagogy and (2) creation of knowledge through research.

Let us start with teaching and pedagogy.

What are the core pedagogic orthodoxies of business education underlying undergraduate or graduate degrees today? And how enabling and/or constraining are they to reimagining and redesigning education programs for the future?

In its current form, for the undergraduate business degree, the basic design philosophy in the United States is a four-year model. This involves some core courses in non-business areas in other departments of the university and exposure to the liberal arts. Mostly, the design is a sequenced set of courses starting with the basics (economics, quantitative methods) and ending with specialized subjects such as strategy, leadership, or advanced finance.

The development of such courses typically involves a course book (with concepts and cases), accompanied by live instruction by a faculty member ("a sage on the stage"), using class sessions to either animate and illustrate concepts and frameworks with different examples or case discussion orchestrated by a faculty member ("a master conductor") to bring out nuances of specific decision contexts.

This model, as we have continually emphasized, has not – in essence – changed much in the last 50 years.

Then come team-based exercises where students work on assigned projects to apply concepts and frameworks to specific situations – for example, the application of strategy frameworks to understand a particular industry and different strategic options or application of accounting concepts to delve deeper into a company's situation.

> There has been increased reliance on global experience visits that some impartial assessments may conclude to be just slightly better than educational tourism

There are also presentations that are aimed to develop useful communications skills where teams of students present (in scripted form) their mastery of concepts and frameworks as applied to specific situations in the form of summary assessments and recommendations.

Graduate programs are advanced versions of similar pedagogical principles for the design and delivery of courses. There can be variations in the form of computer simulations in marketing or organizational behavior or labs in finance intended to provide more hands-on experience of trading or digital technology labs to examine security vulnerabilities.

There has been increased reliance on global experience visits that some impartial assessments may conclude to be just slightly better than educational tourism (uncharitable, of course).

Recent years have seen more discussions on ethics, often sprinkled with high-profile ex-executives who have been fined and/or convicted coming back to campuses and no doubt expressing remorse. Technology has been incrementally adopted, largely supporting traditional efforts.

Clearly there are some variations but the description above is a generally true characterization of the essence of business education. And global accreditation bodies – AACSB, EFMD, and others – have ensured that the different programs meet minimum standards of course and program design.

This includes faculty qualifications, content quality, minimum resources, and overall program design. Each requirement was developed through a historic lens focused on the norms of schools themselves – not the rapidly changing markets in which they operate.

Have the accreditation bodies through their process of granting accreditation guided business schools to minimize risk, embrace greater conformity and isomorphism, and stifle innovations? In many ways, they have. Teaching institutions struggle to support faculty research output; research institutions support revenue-losing doctoral programs, and new ideas are often scrutinized not for merit but for impact on an institution's accreditation and, more broadly, media rankings. In recent years we have seen a strong shift toward assessing outcomes and impact, but will this be enough?

On the topic of accreditation Neil Braun, Dean of Lubin School of Business at Pace University in the United States, remarked during the Jam: "Should accreditation criteria align with the changing needs of employers or academic criteria relating to credit hours and faculty control? How should credit for competencies be treated by accreditation organizations?"

Of course, business schools do not need external pressures to be innovative or adapt to the changing demands of the marketplace. And the Jam made it clear that now is the time to think seriously about reimagining business education.

Here is a thought experiment that is worth engaging with. For this purpose, let us focus on undergraduate business education.

What would be the design of undergraduate business education if we challenged our existing notions and assumptions and discarded them? What if we went back to the proverbial drawing board to design an undergraduate business degree from scratch?

This is precisely what a new initiative, named "30 weeks," is striving to do in New York City. This program is a joint experiment involving Hyper Island, supported by Google in partnership with SVA, Parsons, Pratt, The Cooper Union, and advised by many leading design thinkers including David Kelley, founder of IDEO, and venture capitalists associated with Google ventures.

The focus of this new program is to transform designers into founders. Instead of a traditional curriculum teaching concepts with limited applications (constrained by the resources of traditional schools), this initiative taps into the resource base and networks of Google and venture capitalists to show students a more direct way that connects design thinking to entrepreneurship, namely founding of companies.

Of course, in the past business schools have introduced courses on entrepreneurship, experimented with integrative courses that combined functions, and have also organized business plan competitions judged by external experts and practitioners. These are useful starting points but do they go far enough? Do experiments such as 30 weeks – at the periphery of business school education – threaten us in the short or long term? Perhaps not directly in the immediate future. However, more such experiments could draw highly qualified students away from traditional programs.

The 30-week program is interdisciplinary, a word fraught with problems and challenges within business schools.

Business opportunities and challenges lie at the intersection of boundaries or at the cross-over of functions such as marketing and operations or technology and strategy. Innovations occur at the boundaries of disciplines such as design, marketing, and healthcare. Yet our courses still reflect traditional orthodoxies of a single function or a single discipline.

A higher-education administrator remarked during the Jam: "A brand manager for a large online retailer commented to me recently that he needs employees who have the design sensibilities of an art major coupled with the technical know-how of a computer science major along with the marketing and finance knowledge of a business major."

He also commented, unsurprisingly perhaps, that this combination is incredibly rare and difficult to find.

Is this a case of businesses looking for the "purple squirrel" – a candidate who exists only in the mind of the hiring manager? Or is it reflective of institutions where the walls between art departments, computer science departments, and marketing departments are high and thick?

A recent Chief Technology and Strategy Officer from a NASDAQ 100 company, remarked during the Jam: "Business graduates [who] combine courses in other disciplines are of great value in industry. The challenge for schools is to make business education more interdisciplinary by design rather than by preference."

The key operative phrase is that we need to think of interdisciplinary *by design* on how different courses and themes fit and flow together rather than offering a broad portfolio of courses where students knit together their own program of study – albeit with limited understanding of any grand design.

Going further with the same thought experiment:

What if we innovated and imagined a model of undergraduate business education that did not assume that knowledge assimilation happens in a linear four-year span of sequenced courses made up of core and electives? What if not all business students need to go through the same sequenced logic of instruction – which reflects an industrial-age model of education? What if we could customize the educational experience while maintaining pedagogical integrity?

One Jam participant, pondered that: "It could be that we need to think of the education provided by universities as a much longer-term proposition and much more flexibly organized. If there are more undergraduate business majors because these degrees make it easier to get jobs (to pay off the costs of that education, among other things) then those new job holders should be able to continue studying liberal arts subjects while they are working. The mix of business content, internships, liberal arts courses, mentoring, studying abroad, etc., can be stretched over, say, a 10-year period whereby a student can rely on the university to provide a customized, long-term, and very broad education. Why four years and then you are gone and only graduate study is open to you?"

> Our business model for education, rooted in an outdated model, is unsuited for student-centered mastery of learning and thinking. In other words, we offer standard products and services while students demand tailored solutions

Such personalized and flexible models have been experimented with in other settings – most notably in elementary and high schools. Sal Khan, of Khan Academy fame, has initiated a new experiment with his Khan Lab School "to develop new, personalized practices that center around the student"... and "to develop and test new types of learning experiences and practices that can be shared with the world."

Khan's focus is on mastery of thinking. The experimental philosophy underlying his initiative is interesting in itself – the main focus in all subjects is leveraging world-class teacher-designers to build a community that encourages inquiry and self-direction.

Our business model for education, rooted in an outdated archetype, is unsuited for student-centered mastery of learning and thinking. In other words, we offer standard products and services while students demand tailored solutions.

Industry has recognized the important role of platforms as ways to maintain the efficiency of product design and development while offering ways for individual consumers to customize the use of such products. This is particularly true as innovations evolve from stand-alone designs to digital platforms.

We believe that this platform thinking will serve us well as we reimagine business education. Indeed, we argue that it is the only way to shift from a product-centered view of business education as defined by faculty to a more service-oriented approach. A service orientation connects students, recruiters, alumni, and faculty and the overall design of a business education platform facilitates and rewards for the interactions across the value streams of these different stakeholder.

So, following the logic expressed in Chapter 5, the imperative of the process should involve building out from courses to programs (services) to platforms as a way to open up to new stakeholders and then connect their value streams. This drives more continuous innovation and change that can create new value for each stakeholder and, overall, increase value for all stakeholders. In this way, the evolution of business education to include all three of these layers establishes a healthy ecosystem; a complex network of interactions across different value streams.

Staying with the same thought experiment and applying the analogy of platforms, how could business schools design educational platforms with a set of pedagogical principles that allow for the creation of courses and other learning modules from different participants – including other schools, publishing houses, and even corporate sponsors? This is an initial idea alongside the thought experiment and more promising and powerful ideas could emerge if we let such experiments be conducted at scale.

Moving further with the thought experiment, what if we do not assume that core courses need to be taught first before elective courses? What if the design of education is not subject-focused but problem-centered where the students reach for the concepts when needed to solve specific problems?

What about the core assumptions of pedagogy? What if we assume that faculty members are not the sole authorities of business knowledge? What if we assume that faculty members with superior credentials based on research published in academic journals may not be best suited to teach the practicalities needed to apply them? What if we challenge the assumption that the case method – designed and perfected in the pre-Google age – does not need to be revised and modified for the modern age? What if we challenge the assumption that teachers and learners must be in the same place – especially in this digitally connected world?

Here again, we could imagine what is possible with digital technologies. In the 1990s, business schools designed trading rooms to simulate stock exchanges and other financial markets to give students a real-life feel while studying financial concepts and methods in class. This approach did not extend to other areas such as supply chain and logistics or network operations, mainly for cost reasons; it would have been prohibitive to create mocked-up versions of FedEx hubs or Wal-Mart warehouses.

Now we have the opportunity to take advantage of developments in digital technologies. Google showed a glimpse of what's possible with their Abbey Road project, which lets users virtually explore the three studios with more than 150 different 360-degree panoramic images, YouTube videos and archival images spanning more than 80 years. What if business schools collaborated with Google (or other technology leaders) to develop similar projects that bring together the richness and history of business concepts and cases?

> Is it far-fetched to imagine augmented reality applications to let students immerse themselves as part of supply chains or warehouse operations or design new products or understand the different uses of products in different conditions and cultures?

Along the same lines, what are possible roles for augmented and virtual reality using, for example, Microsoft HoloLens or Facebook Oculus or Google Cardboard? Is it far-fetched to imagine augmented reality applications to let students immerse themselves as part of supply chains or warehouse operations or design new products or understand the different uses of products in different conditions and cultures?

The second orthodoxy is about how we frame the research mission within business schools. As a core element of the business school, research has provided validity but is increasingly questioned, a point raised by Jitendra Singh during the Jam, who commented: "This model of the research-focused business school has diffused widely and this is testimony to its success. However, this battle for legitimacy within the inner confines of academia was largely won by the late 1980s and early 1990s. The issue that has come back with some force is the relevance of what we research and teach in b-schools, and its value to society. This underlies the legitimacy of b-schools as we have known them in the context of broader society."

What are the core orthodoxies of business school research today and how relevant and/or constraining are they to reimagining and redesigning how we create and disseminate knowledge that advances our thinking and practice?

In its current form, the orthodoxy is reflected in how departments within business schools are constituted. It is very common for them to be defined and demarcated along functional lines: marketing, operations, quantitative methods, organization behavior, information systems, finance, accounting, and so on. Such specifications reinforce the hiring and appointment of scholars with doctorates who have been well trained in specific functions often grounded in one of the core disciplines of management – economics, mathematics, psychology, sociology, and information theory.

Although interdisciplinary thinking may advance management thought, the structure of business schools along functional dimensions has inhibited any significant inter- or cross-disciplinary advancement. An additional problem is that most scholarly journals have a strong preference for discipline-based research while interdisciplinary research is generally considered less rigorous.

Most assessments of business schools conclude that the quality and quantity of research output has gone up significantly since the 1960s.

Using conventional criteria such as published articles in peer-reviewed journals we have become respectable in the eyes of our university peers as professional research schools. However, on the question of the impact of our research on practice, the evidence is not so clear cut.

A professor at a leading European Business School remarked during the Jam: "In my own field of strategy, researchers and practitioners have been drifting farther apart [rather] than closer together. Yet, when I raise the topic with my academic colleagues, most see nothing wrong in such indications. Unless corrected, this increasing divergence between business academia and practice is an outcome that the top schools might be able to sustain for a while (especially the ones in the US with large endowments) but that would not be sustainable for lower-ranked schools trying both to climb the research rankings and to build/maintain some connections with business practice."

Implicit in his observations is that ivory tower research may well be justified in the spirit of academic inquiry as long as supported by university funds but that such research may be difficult to fund through research grants from funding agencies or corporations. It is clear that we need a more balanced portfolio of research initiatives. But in searching for academic respectability through research have we forgotten interacting with and influencing practice?

The contribution to the Jam by John Byrne, President and Editor-in-Chief of *Poets & Quants* – an influential blog about business education – was blunt:

> The vast majority of research in business schools is a complete waste of money and time. Most of it has little, if any, use currently or in the future to the practitioner and it is little more than an esoteric exercise designed as part of the performance and reward system to grant tenure. It is being used to justify the notion that a professional school can be scholarly too. Of course, there are some very notable exceptions but they are few and far between. The research game in business academia is one of the big scandals in management education.

Even if we do not believe that the research game is a "scandal" we have to address the relevance and imagine how we could refocus to be more influential. For many years, faculty research in business schools has been heavily cross-subsidized by student tuition, with funded research accounting for only a small fraction.

The rise of for-profit business schools, the proliferation of skill-building content freely available on the internet, and the creation of top-tier research outfits in companies such as Google (marketing and analytics), Goldman Sachs (finance and quantitative models), and Facebook (consumer research) threaten the traditional model of funding business research. The next decade may well compel business schools and universities to rethink how research might be funded. And that could well shift what research projects actually do get funds.

The two major categories of orthodoxies relating to teaching and research have been solidified over the last six decades since the 1959 reports.

While we have made some adjustments and adapted by redesigning courses at the margin or embarked on some relevant research using rigorous methods to inform practice, the ideal solution is when there is alignment between teaching and research. Professional schools should be best at framing contemporary challenges in ways that researchers study and solve them.

Clay Christensen at Harvard Business School remarked that: "Every case we are developing has to be used in the class. And every case has to be coupled with a theory. The result is that there isn't a conflict between the research and teaching."

Although this alignment and harmony may be true in narrow domains, the overwhelming evidence points to a divergent pull between research and teaching.

We must redress this divergence as a core tenet of reimagining the future of business education in the 21st century.

6.1. Three Difficult Questions

As a community of practicing leaders and as academic researchers and teachers, we must confront some thorny questions and make concerted changes going forward well into the 21st century. At the end of the Jam, the authors reviewed, synthesized, and arrived at broad categories of questions that deserve more systematic attention.

As long-established business schools enter their second century and alternatives to traditional offerings emerge, the business education community must address three questions. These are:

> We must go beyond historical thinking and acting as isolated and loosely linked independent institutions and stakeholders

1. **The value question:** Why do business schools exist and what distinctive value do we offer to students, employers, and the world at large?
2. **The learning question:** How do we coach the next generation of students to learn the skills and perspectives of business against the backdrop of alternative ways to access high-quality content, including online?

3. **The relevance and impact of research question:** How should business schools organize their research mission to develop and disseminate insights to influence leading-edge practice?

The questions may not be new as they have been distilled from the discussions during the Jam. More important is the way that we must address these questions. We must go beyond historical thinking and acting as isolated and loosely linked independent institutions and stakeholders. We call for addressing these questions using the ideas of platforms and ecosystems.

6.1.1. WHAT IS THE DISTINCTIVE VALUE OF BUSINESS SCHOOLS?

Why do business schools exist? What is our distinctive value? These questions may have a simple answer.

Business schools exist to create and disseminate relevant knowledge to students and educate and prepare managers capable of dealing with important problems facing the world.

Sure, we can wordsmith the above answer; the essence is that business schools exist to deliver value to students, employers, and society.

6.1.1.1. Value to students

More than at any other time in history, the economic value of business education is now questioned – especially for MBAs. While the elite institutions may provide easy payback, it may not be true for all MBA programs. The duration of programs (typically two years for an MBA in the United States) also weighs heavily in the value equation for US programs. Non-US programs have demonstrated value with shorter programs (e.g., INSEAD's one-year program). The availability of online content through digital sources (such as MOOCs) also influences the value equation, as does the emergence of specialized masters programs.

6.1.1.2. Value to employers

Ultimately, students see the value of business education when employers see business graduates with the right set of skills and capabilities to tackle the challenges of the business world.

Employers expect graduates from business schools to be effective managers and competent leaders.

New graduates are expected to have mastered hard skills (concepts, theories, and frameworks) balanced with soft skills (influence, teamwork, and communication). They should have depth in specific functional areas while having the broader perspective to see the proverbial "big picture."

While they must know the intricacies of theories, more importantly they should be able apply them to solve problems efficiently and in a global environment with appropriate competences in cultural and contextual intelligence.

They should be deft in using the latest computer tools and analytical models yet make informed judgments and convince their colleagues and others of the veracity of their decisions.

To the extent that business education prepares students with such mastery of skills and capabilities, we deliver value to employers; in turn, we deliver value to the students.

6.1.1.3. Value for the world

Through their research and teaching, business schools must address the complex problems of society. How do we tackle the issues of insufficient global healthcare, economic inequality, food insecurity, climate change, and sustainability? Are we devoting sufficient attention and resources to address such problems or are we content with making incremental contributions to established domains of management research?

For the better part of the last 50 years we have primarily focused our research on problems faced by the private, for-profit sectors of the economy. As such, business thinking has not permeated into other sectors of the economy – including healthcare, cities and governments, environment, energy, infrastructure, etc. Our research – especially multidisciplinary thinking – must be brought to bear to increase efficiency and create greater value to the world in the coming decades.

6.1.2. WHAT SHOULD BE THE DISTINCTIVE PEDAGOGY OF BUSINESS SCHOOLS?

How do we guide the next generation of students (millennials) to learn? Can we shift our focus from teaching to coaching and facilitating? What should be the relative mix of content in business school – skills versus perspectives?

Over the last five decades, business schools have developed methods to teach skills – in the form of core courses that deal with traditional models and theories (statistics, information systems, accounting, finance, decision making, etc.) and applications of those skills through integrative courses in marketing, strategy, and others. We have refined consistent methods for teaching those skills through textbooks and problem sets. As do law schools, we have relied on the case method for teaching the application of skills in different decision contexts.

Historically, the competing pulls and tensions in business school pedagogy have been between concepts and cases – what should be the relative mix of formally derived normative models and rules versus emergent insights through discussions of complex cases?

Going forward, the debate should be between the emphasis on deep skills and broad perspectives. This is particularly timely because of the growing availability of online resources for skills. Campus-based learning is less about the delivery of standard concepts, theories, and frameworks by expert faculty and more about helping each student connect the different concepts, apply them to solve problems, and show interconnections across problems in broader, dynamic systems.

In other words, the model of pedagogy shifts from teaching to learning. The role of faculty shifts from delivering content to coaching to bring out nuances that are best discovered through discussions, dialogue, and classroom debates.

> Historically, the competing pulls and tensions in business school pedagogy have been between concepts and cases – what should be the relative mix of formally derived normative models and rules versus emergent insights through discussions of complex cases?

MOOCs are modern-era textbooks delivered and curated by experts. They are efficient and effective in accessing standard content (skills). Mastery of business education involves skills and perspectives; the latter can only be achieved through social and intellectual interactions among peers, facilitated by faculty acting as coaches.

Santiago Iñiguez de Onzoño, Dean of IE Business School and the President of IE University, commented during the Jam: "A recurrent issue is whether technology would reduce the costs of education, particularly at business schools. Many analysts predicted that MOOCs would contribute to substantial costs reductions in the delivery of programs. Has this been the case? Not yet. The production and delivery costs of Moocs are potentially high, ranging from $3,000 – for very basic courses – up to $250,000. Given that MOOCs do not replace traditional degrees, the costs or running MOOCs at universities have to be added to those of implementing existing regular programs."

Is it possible to design cost-effective programs where the skills are learned through accredited MOOCs (supported by exams) and a campus focused on discussions, dialogs, and debates to understand the concepts as applied and connected to other ideas?

We believe that this core idea holds promise but the approach requires us to collaborate as a community and arrive at new models of pedagogy. MOOCs are starting points. They should be seen as complementary to business education and not substitutes.

6.1.3. WHAT SHOULD BE THE DISTINCTIVE RESEARCH CONTRIBUTIONS OF BUSINESS SCHOOLS?

We have already discussed the orthodoxy in how we approach research within business schools. Our role as creators of relevant knowledge that impacts practice is under attack. As *The Economist* puts it:

Business professors often still view themselves as the campus underdogs and, keen to boost their credibility, tend to favour dry topics to impress academics in other disciplines, rather than finding practical applications for their ideas. Criticism of how business schools may have helped create the end of the business world as we know it would seem to echo Gordon-Howell's point about the need for more emphasis on ethics. And the likes of the collapse of Enron also tend to loom large in the minds of critics of business morals. (*The Economist*, 2009)

> Since business school research is often considered as "derivative" or "applied," many faculty members work hard to make their work more theoretical in order to be recognized by the high priests of the disciplines

The Business Education Jam generated a lot of discussions with diverse viewpoints pertaining to ethics. Strong support emerged for serious, deep reform of ethical leadership teaching in the classroom, which could ultimately have long-lasting impact on the world. However, we are far from developing a coherent set of approaches to the study and research of ethics within business schools – admittedly complex and multi-faceted.

Business research has been narrower within functions and disciplines. In advancing fundamental theories in disciplines, business school researchers tend to benchmark their work against researchers in relevant discipline-based departments in universities such as economics, psychology, sociology, computer sciences, and mathematics.

It is not uncommon for psychology researchers to be in a university's liberal arts department of psychology in addition to being within business schools in departments such as marketing (consumer behavior), organization behavior (leadership), strategy (decision theory), and economics (behavioral economics).

Business school researchers trained as psychologists assess their contributions relative to other business school faculty as well as those in other relevant areas of psychology within the university. Since business school research is often considered as "derivative" or "applied," many faculty members work hard to make their work more theoretical in order to be recognized by the high priests of the disciplines.

In the future business school researchers may find themselves competing for attention with corporate research departments, consulting organizations, and free-standing research institutions. During the 1980s some felt that the best finance departments were within Wall Street institutions – which attracted researchers working on different models and applications. But the same did not happen in other functions or disciplines.

Strategy frameworks, theories, and rules emerged from Harvard Business School in the 1980s and the consulting companies adapted them into their strategy practices. Marketing models and frameworks emerged from scholars at Kellogg and Wharton and operations research ideas came from MIT and Carnegie Mellon, and so on.

Now, there is some concern that new companies such as Google, Facebook, Twitter, Yahoo, Uber and others are at the forefront of research that is at the core of their product/service platform offerings.

These companies have attracted talented faculty from universities – for example, Duncan Watts, a noted researcher on networks, is at Microsoft; Hal Varian, previously the Dean of Berkeley School of Information, is at Google; Joel Podolny, previously Dean at Yale School of Management, is at Apple University. Looking outside of business schools, Uber has hired robotics researchers away from Carnegie-Mellon University.

These could be isolated instances. However, the implications are clear: if business schools start to lose their stars to industry research labs they may find themselves caught in being (1) seen as applied researchers by those located within disciplinary departments; (2) not seen as top-tier locales for cutting-edge research as compared to industry.

Even so, business schools are working to connect faculty with industry. Sri Zaheer, Dean at the Carlson School of Management at Minnesota in the US, remarked during the Jam: "We have just begun to try and connect faculty members one-on-one with a senior executive – often an alum – or with a firm that shares the faculty member's interests. It is not easy to find good pairings, but when you get a good connection, it works like magic ..."

Although there are many other initiatives to foster connections, as long as faculty are rewarded for publications in academic journals they are unlikely to look at such linkages as anything more than institutional service activities.

One faculty member during the Jam remarked: "We teach companies to be ambidextrous but rarely practice it. Ambidextrous scholars publish in both the top journals but also publish the key insights of their research in practitioner's outlets for broader audiences." Unfortunately such scholars are few and far between.

We need to go from such isolated instances to think of research that drives practice at scale. We believe that adding the service (programs) and platform layers to business school education is the means of developing a value-creating ecosystem and is the most promising way forward.

6.2. Toward a Business Education Platform and Ecosystem for the 21st Century

The Jam was designed as an online platform for conversations involving multiple different stakeholders on a global scale.

The discussions, insights, and implications at the end of the Jam come back to the same core idea – we need a platform for further innovation.

The global world of business has evolved to be interconnected and networked. At the same time, business schools are mostly independent institutions in their twin roles of teaching and research. Little formal collaboration exists across institutions on a systematic basis (beyond informal collaborations and professional connections between faculty members). Sure, there are bilateral programs for joint degrees across institutions but those are not true cross-institutional collaborations.

Even collaboration between business schools and industry is *ad hoc*. As the Dean of the Carlson School of Management commented earlier, every dean could point to his or her own ways of collaborating with companies in the form of custom-curated programs, specific research projects, live case competitions, course projects, and so on.

Even in research activities, business schools operate mostly independently. Rare are multi-school, multi-year projects that deal with big, audacious problems and challenges. Reward systems reinforce individuals' research contributions and not institutional contributions. Hence, it is not surprising that we have continued to operate in isolation.

We started this chapter focused on the twin orthodoxies pertaining to teaching and research and asked a set of "what if" questions to reimagine our ability to teach and do research.

We end the chapter with a thought experiment meant to spur actions on our part.

Let us start with the following question: What would the model of business education be if we embraced the core logic of a platform? Just as the platform model redefined the software business from stand-alone products and services, what if business education was a platform that had a core operating system with modules contributed by different schools and different companies?

Platforms are powerful when supported by strong network effects: To begin with, we need a broad cross-section of course modules. The analogy with the software platform is that Windows succeeded with support from software developers that made its modules work on a Windows platform. Windows was attractive to end users because of the strength of compatible software titles. The interplay between direct- and indirect-network effects helped Windows to succeed. So, Windows and the ecosystem participants worked to co-create the platform that unleashed significant value in the pc industry. The same logic is in play now with Android and Apple with their respective app stores. Platforms that facilitate and reward the interaction of many stakeholders provide the key building blocks of a business education ecosystem.

So, our thought experiment about platform and ecosystem for business school education could go along the following lines.

Today, we have strong products and weak services.

What would that platform look like? What would be the guiding principles for designing such a platform? How would a platform reshape products and services? What could be the principles for governing such a platform so that all business schools shared it?

This represents a significant evolutionary challenge, and an opportunity to be missed at our own peril for those of us involved in providing business education. Together, we must reimagine business education.

> Just as the platform model redefined the software business from standalone products and services, what if business education was a platform that had a core operating system with modules contributed by different schools and different companies?

7 Next Steps: Where Do We Go from Here?

A shifting landscape could have heralded ground-breaking innovation in business education during the past 50 years. Unfortunately, it has not. This lack of innovation in turn reflects resource constraints among differing cultures and to differing degrees around the world. Asian management education, for example, is diverse and heterogeneous and has its own context and priorities; India, for its part, struggles with a shortage of qualified faculty; while China faces constraints in academic autonomy.

The sometimes forgotten continent of Africa faces a huge educational challenge in developing and upskilling managers to fulfill its long-term economic growth and societal/infrastructure investment.

Clearly, there are many dilemmas that exist in addressing the future of business schools and business education. The Business Education Jam highlighted challenges and yielded context and a set of ideas for addressing them. The Jam also generated a series of questions that business school deans may choose to avoid, but these questions will not go away. How we address them will be tremendously enriched if they are solved through the lens of a new, service-oriented "platform" and "ecosystem for business education" rather than a traditional "product" focus.

1. How does a business school innovate and if it does, what is the nature of the innovation process in a business school? Is it a series of small innovations that accumulate to a logical, larger whole or rather the result of a large disruption, as suggested by writers such as Clayton Christensen?

2. How do business school deans lead? What is the nature of the strategic leadership process in business schools? There is plenty of evidence to suggest conservatism and inertia in the actions of many business school deans. Few studies have examined this process, a notable exception being the work of Fraguiero and Thomas (Cambridge University Press, 2011).

3. Where does management research offer distinctive insights to guide policy and practice? The ongoing concern about the widening gap between cutting-edge research and management practice means the issue of a lack of multi-disciplinarity in research looms large, particularly when we examine research issues such as innovation, crisis management, and the alleviation of poverty.

4. Can we teach management at scale? What is the future of IT-enabled learning and the dilemmas faced in handling MOOCs and blended learning approaches to management education? For example, it is clear in the African context that the major improvement in management education is to educate at scale a population of managers (approximately one million) who have little or no university education or formal management training.

5. How do we engage industry actively? There is a dilemma around how to handle student-centered participative learning, which inevitably requires both close collaboration with business and industry and smaller class sizes in which to facilitate the learning process. This has strong implications for the funding model of business schools, particularly the ability to scale programs and hire high-quality faculty. In addition, we need a dynamic model of engagement with business school research beyond a passive hands-off approach.

6. How quickly should we move beyond Western models of management thinking and teaching? There is a dilemma and a tension between globalization in the management

education field and the need for clear local differentiation of curricula and learning approaches in different cultures and contexts. We call this the "glocalisation" dilemma.

7. What are new frames of legitimacy of the role and contribution of business schools as central institutions? There is continuing debate in academic circles about the legitimacy of business schools: are they learning organizations, following the idea of the university offered by Cardinal Newman, or are they simply "wastelands of vocationalism," to use a term coined by Herbert Simon?

The Business Education Jam conducted by Boston University Questrom School of Business and partnering organizations was a vital first step in bringing industry and academia together to identify a path forward to help insure relevance, reach and respect for business schools for years to come. Much more needs to be done by each business school, and as a collective. Toward that end, the Questrom School of Business, in collaboration with academic, organizational, and industry partners, intends to continue championing the dialogue with broadened geographic and industry participation, to insure that all voices are heard.

We are at the beginning of a transformational journey. Let's reimagine business education, together.

Postscript: Ensuring Relevance, Reach, and Respect

To continue to survive and prosper, business education needs to do several things: (1) institute quality control standards to reduce the proliferation of dodgy providers chasing enrollments and tuition using, on occasion, boiler-room tactics – a condition that offers reputational risk to virtually all providers of business training; (2) make the educational, developmental aspects of business training front and center and de-emphasize the assessment of programs primarily by whether or not they raise their graduates' salaries, a standard that other professional programs do not so doggedly embrace; (3) as part of a renewed emphasis on education, address issues of student culture and misbehavior, particularly in the full-time, residential programs where networking and partying leave business school students less engaged with their schoolwork than their peers in other disciplines; and (4) make at least some effort to systematically assess, as the Aspen Institute has done on occasion, the effect of business education on ethics and values, as well as possibly on what students learn and their attitudes as a consequence of partaking of the business school experience.

On the first point, with more than 13,000 purveyors of business education programs, fewer than 10% of which are accredited, and with many rankings and discussions of business schools primarily emphasizing their salary-enhancing outcomes, business education is for the most part more about revenues and enrollments than anything else. This leaves business programs ill-suited to credibly claim much attention to ethics and values beyond the window-dressing efforts undertaken occasionally in response to financial and other scandals.

Other knowledgeable observers, including former Yale dean Joel Podolny, former Harvard Business School professor Rakesh Khurana, and the late Sumantra Ghoshal have made similar arguments, thus far with little effect.

On the second point, other professional schools, such as law, medicine, and engineering, obviously need to place their graduates. But few, maybe none, measure whether or not they have succeeded with as narrow a focus as business schools. Law schools worry about the proportion of students who get jobs and bar passage rates, and medical schools often emphasize whether or not their graduates have been trained in the science of medicine to ensure good residencies and also their ability to continue to learn. Business schools emphasize money much more than other programs, possibly to their detriment.

Residential business education programs in particular often have lax policies with respect to alcohol, partying, and academic performance. Not surprisingly, what evidence there is suggests lower levels of academic engagement by business school students than their counterparts from other disciplines and occasional scandals that question the legitimacy of the business school enterprise.

Higher education generally, and business schools more specifically, for the most part resist doing much systematic assessment of what happens to people who attend them – with the possible exception of tracking salary increases. The Aspen Institute and Ghoshal, among others, have on occasion been concerned with the attitudes and values that are affected by business school ideology and training. But for the most part, what effects business education has on ethics, values, beliefs, and attitudes may form the subject of an occasional research project but is not much part of systematic assessments. Such neglect belies both the incredible size of the business education enterprise and its possible effects on student and indeed society-wide thinking.

In short, my recommendations for what business education should do derive logically from the fact that in many countries, business majors at both the undergraduate and post-graduate levels are among the most numerous of all fields of study, business education is truly big business, and what studies there are suggest an effect of business education on attitudes and values of its students. As a socially important area of study, business education should take its responsibilities more seriously, doing a better job of overseeing its numerous purveyors to provide some level of quality control and being more attentive to the numerous, multidimensional effects of business training on society.

Jeffrey Pfeffer
Thomas D. Dee II Professor of Organizational Behavior,
Graduate School of Business, Stanford University

Appendix A

Business Education Jam Sponsors

The Business Education Jam was not possible without the support, engagement, and encouragement from our sponsoring organizations.

Presented by

Boston University Questrom School of Business

In collaboration with

Additional support provided by

Appendix B

The 10 Forums of the Business Education Jam

Discussion Forum Label 1	**Supporting 21st Century Competencies**
Tagline	Educating a global workforce
Key question	How can academia and industry collaborate to identify and support the development of critical competencies?
Short description	Today's global economy requires a changing array of knowledge, skills, and competencies. Which competencies are needed by industry and how will academia respond to these new requirements? How will academia maintain relevance by co-innovating with industry (instead of being independent)?
Long description	When asked in the 2014 Gallup/Lumina Foundation poll, only 11% of business leaders strongly agreed that higher education institutions in the United States are graduating students with the skills and competencies that businesses need. Business schools need to collaborate more closely with industry to understand what companies are looking for in their next hires. In the classroom and in the world, business education must arm students with the knowledge and experience that will translate seamlessly to their careers. Not all training happens on the job. It happens during college, too.

Discussion Forum Label 2	Increasing the Value of Management Education
Tagline	Opportunities across all levels of learning
Key question	How can management education programs enhance value for students, employers, and industry?
Short description	Challenges to value are rising across all levels of education. What is the role of management education as a first or second degree? How will the emergence of specialized programs impact the MBA? How will management education change to provide increased value to stakeholders?
Long description	The amount of applicants to MBA programs is dropping. As is the percentage of MBAs who considered their graduate education a "good to outstanding value," according to GMAC's 2014 Alumni Perspectives Survey. With the job market still struggling to make a comeback, recent graduates are questioning whether their first degree was even worth it. Business education needs a boost. It needs the input of all stakeholders to increase its relevance and discover how to better prepare students to be efficient, effective, and successful in the workforce. Business schools must be a place where students gain a competitive edge that lands them a job – and keeps them ahead of the pack.

Discussion Forum Label 3	**Engaging New-Generation Students and Employees**
Tagline	Challenges and opportunities of a millennial generation
Key question	How will industry and business education tap the unlimited potential of millennials?
Short description	Today's innovative generation will change industry and education. How will industry attract the brightest employees and graduates to management professions? How will schools educate the millennials (born digital and living/ learning social), and how will industry cultivate and retain them?
Long description	According to the U.S. Census Bureau, in 2013, there were more 22-year-olds in the United States than any other age. The millennials have overtaken the baby boomers and are positioned to overtake the economy as well. Business schools must evolve to fit the needs of this dynamic generation to prepare them for their rising prominence. More experiential learning and a stronger global focus are a just two of the areas that require greater innovation in business education so that students are graduating with the skills they need to impact our shifting world.

Discussion Forum Label 4	**Cultivating Research Relevance and Rigor**
Tagline	Collaborative research across industry and academia
Key question	How will management research drive insights for industry best practices?
Short description	The research landscape is changing. How can management research be better aligned to shape and influence management practice? How can research relevance be enhanced while maintaining rigor? How can academia engage thought leaders in industry as research collaborators using digital technologies?
Long description	Future best practices will not be "best" if academics simply talk to academics. Their conversations must break out of silos and engage all stakeholders affected by their work. Through greater collaboration with industry, business schools will tap into the kind of studies, numbers, and data that have the ability to shape how management functions. Thought leaders can better grasp what direction in which to focus their research — and how best to distribute it — for increased relevance and reach. Improved business research leads to improved business performance. To achieve this, uniting both sides is critical.

Discussion Forum Label 5	**Fostering Ethical Leadership**
Tagline	Advancing ethics, character, and integrity
Key question	How can ethical leadership be fostered across business education and industry?
Short description	There is an increased focus on ethics from industry and the academy. What role should management schools and universities play in teaching ethics? What is the role of life-long learning in fostering ethical leadership? How can academia work with industry to broaden the understanding of ethical dilemmas in a global context? What is the next-generation frontier of research on ethics within management schools?
Long description	Corporate social responsibility stems from personal social responsibility. Business schools must find a way to instill a sense of duty and conviction in their students so that when a decision arises that could affect the culture or fate of a company, they are prepared to make the right one. With collaborations from those on the frontlines of industry – those who have been faced with real moral dilemmas – we can gain a better understanding of what should be taught in the classroom to support ethical leaders. Students should be armed with an outward perspective, considering their impact on the people around them, before they enter their careers. If they are focused only inward, they cannot truly make a difference.

Discussion Forum Label 6	**Cultivating Innovation and Entrepreneurship**
Tagline	Industry and academia collaboratively building an innovation engine
Key question	How will future entrepreneurial leaders be developed?
Short description	Innovation drives growth. What is the collective role of industry and academic in innovation and entrepreneurship? How can the next-generation of global business innovations come from industry and the academia working jointly? Could next-generation entrepreneurs emerge from management schools rather than in "garages?" What facets of entrepreneurship can be taught? Which are learned?
Long description	According to a GMAC's 2014 Alumni Perspectives Survey, almost half (45%) of self-employed respondents who graduated from 2010 to 2013 started their business immediately after graduation, compared to 24% of self-employed MBAs who graduated between 2000 and 2009. More than ever, small business concepts and startup ideas are on the minds of up-and-coming management leaders. Nurturing students' unique ideas in the classroom – and offering them experiential learning opportunities to further their knowledge and skills to carry these ideas out – is essential. Hearing from businesspeople who have taken the entrepreneurial path about what they wish they had known at the start, as well as what they learned along the way, can have a direct influence on how business schools shape their curriculum and ultimately shape the next great innovators.

Discussion Forum Label 7	**Driving Learning Experiences**
Tagline	Impactful learning across industry and education
Key question	How can business education and industry collaboratively impact student learning?
Short description	Learning today comes in many forms. How can schools enhance student engagement and their educational experiences? How can schools better collaborate to enhance student engagement with industry? How can new models of experiential learning complement traditional modes of learning in classrooms? What innovative learning experiences are occurring within industry?
Long description	According to the 2014 Gallup/Lumina Foundation poll, only 9% of business leaders say that a candidate's alma mater is a major factor, and just 28% say the candidate's college major is a very important factor, while 84% say that knowledge in the field is critical in the hiring process. Employers need better graduates, ones who are ready to tackle a complex and demanding economy. This means more field seminars, internships, and hands-on opportunities for students. Together, academia and industry can construct a better approach to student learning so that graduates are getting experience in the real world – before they enter it.

Discussion Forum Label 8	Harnessing Digital Technology
Tagline	Enhancing industry, education, and research
Key question	How will management education and research reflect the digital age?
Short description	Digital technology impacts everything. How can we research and teach with digital technologies? How will academia design management education and research activities for the digital age? How will academia work with industry to bring updated context and data to classrooms and learning/ teaching methods?
Long description	When San Jose State University ran a test course online in electrical engineering, students who worked with online content passed at a higher rate than classroom-only students, 91 to 60%. MOOCs and other online learning opportunities are making waves and forcing higher education to rethink its place in a digital world. Perhaps it's about teaching students better coding and social media skills. Or maybe it's about offering more access to online education. Either way, adapting to continually evolving technology is crucial for business schools and their #1 customers – students. In order for graduates to become successful leaders in today's economy, they can no longer simply be marketers or consultants; they have to be technologists as well. Business schools must effectively prepare them to speak a digital language. To do so, business education must be fluent, too, updating their approaches to teaching and research, and embracing the MOOC model.

Discussion Forum Label 9	Challenging the Business Model of Education
Tagline	Responding to new demands
Key question	How will management education be positioned and funded in the future?
Short description	There exists tremendous pressure on existing business models. What is the business model for management institutions in the future? How should management institutions be funded and operated? How will institutions maintain academic independence while enhancing value for industry through relevant research? How should academia work with other stakeholders going forward (funding agencies, governments, consulting organizations, for-profit universities, online educational models, etc.)?
Long description	A *Wall Street Journal* article reports that since 1990, the cost of attending college has increased at four times the rate of inflation. Meanwhile, student loan debt is approaching $1 trillion. And half of recent college graduates don't have jobs or don't use their degree in the jobs they find. Academia needs to remedy this situation – and fast. To stay relevant and valuable, higher education must look at itself like a business and enhance its relationship with its customers: offer MOOCs and other online learning opportunities, develop programs for different markets, reduce overhead, and more. How can higher education begin to look at itself as a business? By collaborating with businesspeople themselves.

Discussion Forum Label 10	Advancing Policy and Governance
Tagline	Focusing on regulation and rankings
Key question	How will policy and accreditation influence the development of business education and business?
Short description	Business, and concurrently the education of business leaders, impacts most aspects of life for people across the globe. Policy, accreditation and governance shape the direction and perception of schools and businesses and touch a myriad of areas from ethical leadership to cost/benefit relationships. A thorough understanding of the challenges and triumphs of business education and the partnerships between academia and industry will inform policy decisions that have the power to shape the future leaders of our global economy.
Long description	From price tag to access to global impact, policymaking has a far-reaching effect on business schools. Consider the Institute for Higher Education Policy (IHEP), a nonpartisan, nonprofit organization committed to promoting access to and success in higher education for all students. IHEP develops innovative policy- and practice-oriented research that guides education leaders and informs public policy decisions. The Jam shares the same vision, aiming to unite academia and industry to evaluate the business education model and generate relevant research that prompts solutions to issues that need improvement, such as cost, access, and sustainability.

Appendix C

Summary of Jam Participation

Total Business Education Jam Participation Statistics

As reported by the IBM Jam Program Office

24,858 total visits
122 countries represented
157,253 page views
3,969 registrants at the launch of the Business Education Jam
5,730 registrants at the conclusion of the Business Education Jam
44% increase in registrations during the Jam
8,495 total logins
74% registration conversion rate
3,921 unique users
1,258 unique posters

Posts by Discussion Forums: 6,310 Posts

Supporting 21st Century Competencies	1,013
Increasing the Value of Management Education	821
Cultivating Innovation & Entrepreneurship	821
Challenging the Business Model of Education	750
Engaging New-Generation Students & Employees	702
Fostering Ethical Leadership	600
Driving Learning Experiences	483
Producing Research with Impact	428
Harnessing Digital Technology	403
Evaluating Policy & Rankings	289

Post and Login Demographic Information

By Affiliation:

Unique logins by primary affiliation:
Higher Ed Business School with 37% followed by Student 26% and Industry 13%

Total posts by primary affiliation:
Higher Ed Business School with nearly 59% followed by Student at 14% and Industry at 10%

By Location:

Unique logins by country/location: the United States with 69% followed by the United Kingdom at 5% and Mexico/Canada/Thailand/India at 2%

Total posts by country/location:
The United States with 76% followed by the United Kingdom at 4% and Mexico/Canada at 2%

By Position:

Unique logins by position: Student: Current Undergraduate at 27% with Higher Ed: Staff & Administration at 10% and Student: Current graduate at 7%

Total posts by position: Higher Ed: Staff and Administration at 16% followed by Student: Current Undergraduate at 14%

By Gender and Age:

Unique logins by gender and age:
Female 18−21 leads with 15% followed by Male 18−21 with 11% and Female 26−32 at 8%

Total posts by gender and age:
Female 26−32/Male 56−60/Male 33−40 all at 8%

5,730 REGISTRANTS

122 *COUNTRIES*

40+ *INDUSTRIES*

350 *ACADEMIC INSTITUTIONS*

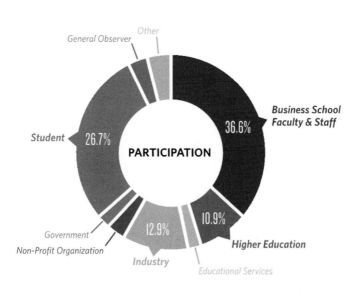

PARTICIPATION

General Observer

Other

Business School Faculty & Staff
36.6%

Student 26.7%

10.9%
Higher Education

12.9%

Government

Non-Profit Organization

Industry

Educational Services

ENGAGEMENT

24,858 ↺
VISITS

157,253 🔍
PAGE VIEWS

6,310 📄
TOTAL POSTS

Appendix D

Business Education Jam VIP Guests

Titles reflect those provided at the time of the Business Education Jam

Anant Agarwal, PhD	CEO, edX, Professor of Electrical Engineering and Computer Science, MIT
Maryam Alavi, PhD	Dean, Stephen P. Zelnak Jr. Chair, Professor of Information Technology Management, Georgia Tech Scheller College of Business
Andrea Backman, PhD	Senior Vice President & Dean, Jack Welch Management Institute
Douglas L. Becker	Chairman & CEO, Laureate Education, Inc.
Sean M. Belka	Senior Vice President and Director of the Fidelity Center for Applied Technology, Fidelity Investments
Ben M. Bensaou, PhD	Professor of Technology and Operations Management, Professor of Asian Business and Comparative Management, INSEAD
Della Bradshaw	Business Education Editor, *Financial Times*
Neil S. Braun, JD	Dean, Lubin School of Business, Pace University
Arthur Brooks, PhD	President, American Enterprise Institute
Robert A. Brown, PhD	President, Boston University
Matthew Burr	CEO & Co-Founder, Nomadic Learning

John A. Byrne	President, Editor in Chief, Poets & Quants
Jacob Chacko, PhD	Dean, College of Business Administration, Abu Dhabi University
Rick Chavez	Chief Solutions Officer, Microsoft Advertising and Consumer Monetization Business Group
Youngsuk Chi	Chairman, Elsevier, President, International Publishers Association
Sangeet Chowfla	President & CEO, Graduate Management Admission Council
Clayton M. Christensen	DBA Kim B. Clark Professor of Business Administration, Harvard Business School
James Ciriello	Associate Vice President, IT Planning & Innovation at Merck & Co.
L. Kevin Cox	Chief Human Resources Officer, American Express Company
Steve Denning	*Forbes* contributor, Board Member of the Scrum Alliance
Deborah Dugan, JD	CEO, RED
Soumitra Dutta, PhD	Anne and Elmer Lindseth Dean, Professor of Management and Organizations, Cornell University
Ceree Eberly	Senior Vice President and Chief People Officer, The Coca-Cola Company
Wafa El Garah, PhD	Dean, School of Business Administration, Al Akhawayn University
Tamara J. Erickson	Founder & CEO, Tammy Erickson Associates
Michael J. Fenlon, PhD	US & Global Talent Leader, PricewaterhouseCoopers
Todd Fisher	Member & Chief Administrative Officer, KKR
Fernando J. Fragueiro, PhD	President, Austral University

Barbara Franklin	President & CEO, Barbara Franklin Enterprises, Former US Secretary of Commerce
David A. Garvin, PhD	C. Roland Christensen Professor of Business Administration, Harvard Business School
Mary C. Gentile, PhD	Director, Giving Voice to Values, Senior Research Scholar, Babson College, Senior Advisor, Aspen Institute
Pankaj Ghemawat, PhD	Anselmo Rubiralta Professor of Global Strategy, IESE Business School, Distinguished Visiting Professor of Global Management, Stern School of Business, New York University
Marshall Goldsmith, PhD	Executive Leadership Coach, Marshall Goldsmith Group
Vijay Govindarajan, PhD	Coxe Distinguished Professor, Dartmouth College's Tuck School of Business
Donald E. Graham	Chairman of the Board and Chief Executive Officer, Graham Holdings
Thierry Grange	President of the Strategic Board, Grenoble Ecole De Management
Lynda Gratton, PhD	Professor of Management Practice, London Business School, Founder of The Hot Spots Movement
Daniel Greenstein, DPhil	Director – Postsecondary Success Strategy, Bill & Melinda Gates Foundation
Jonas Haertle	DBA Head, Principles for Responsible Management Education (PRME) secretariat, UN Global Compact Office
Adolf Ho	CEO, Classic Management Consultants Ltd, Associate Adjunct Professor of Marketing, Hong Kong University of Science and Technology, Past CEO, Campbell Soup Greater China, Vice Chairman, Campbell Soup Shanghai Trading Ltd.

Ulrich Hommel, PhD	Professor of Finance in the Department of Finance & Accounting, Endowed Chair of Corporate Finance & Higher Education Finance, Director of the Strategic Finance Institute, EBS Business School, Director of Research & Surveys, Senior Advisor in the Quality Services Department, EFMD
Jeanette Horan	Managing Director, IBM Corporation
Mel Horwitch, PhD	Dean and University Professor, Central European University Business School
Santiago Iñiguez de Onzoño, PhD	President, IE University, Dean, IE Business School
Martha Josephson	Partner, Digital Media Global Practice Leader, Egon Zehnder
Ashwini Kakkar, PhD	Vice Chairman, Mercury Travels, Chairman of Via.com, Ambit Corporation and the Fight Hunger Foundation
Sherif H. Kamel, Ph. D	Former Dean, School of Business at the American University in Cairo
Assylbeck Kozhakhmetov, DBA	Rector of International Business Academy
Paul J. LeBlanc, PhD	President, University of Southern New Hampshire
Dan LeClair, PhD	Executive Vice President and Chief Operating Officer, AACSB International
Seung-Han Lee, PhD	Next and Partners Chairman, Former Samsung Corporation President and CEO, Former Homeplus CEO and Chairman
Joe Lipuma, DBA	Author, Educator, Commentator
Xiongwen Lu, PhD	Dean of the School of Management, Fudan University
Richard K. Lyons, PhD	Dean, Haas School of Business, University of California, Berkeley

Roger Martin	Premier's Chair in Productivity & Competitiveness and Academic Director, Martin Prosperity Institute at the Rotman School of Management
Jamie P. Merisotis	President and CEO, Lumina Foundation
Vineet Nayar, DBA	Founder, Sampark Foundation, Former CEO, HCL Technologies
Martin A. Nisenholtz	Former Chief Digital Officer, The New York Times Company
Pamela Norley, JD	Executive Vice President of Fidelity's Enterprise Relationships and Talent Groups, Fidelity Investments
John North	Director of Global Operations, Globally Responsible Leadership Initiative
Ramon O'Callaghan, DBA	Dean, Graduate School of Business, Nazarbayev University CAMAN – Central Asian Foundation for Management Development
George Pappas	Chancellor, Victoria University
Ambi M. G. Parameswaran, PhD	Advisor, FCB Ulka Advertising, one of India's largest marketing communication companies; Author of six books; Member Board of Governors, Indian Institute of Management Calcutta
Guy Pfeffermann	Founder & CEO Global Business School Network
James Post, PhD	John F. Smith, Jr. Professors in Management, Boston University Questrom School of Business
Claire Preisser	Senior Program Manager, Business and Society, The Aspen Institute
JP Rangaswami	Chief Scientist, salesforce.com
Ajit Rangnekar	Dean, Indian Business School
Ananth Rao, PhD	Chief Academic Officer, Professor, University of Dubai

Rebecca L. Ray, PhD	Executive Vice President, Knowledge Organization and Human Capital Practice Lead, The Conference Board
John B. Reid-Dodick, JD	Chief People Officer, Dun & Bradstreet Corp.
Max Reinhardt	Worldwide President at DePuy Synthes Spine Companies, Johnson & Johnson
Matthew Robb	Partner, The Parthenon Group
Peter Rohan	Partner, Ernst & Young
Johan Roos, PhD	Dean, CEO and Managing Director, Jönköping International Business School (JIBS)
Michael Salinger, PhD	Jacqueline J. and Arthur S. Bahr Professor in Management, Markets, Public Policy and Law, Boston University Questrom School of Business, Former Director of Bureau of Economics, Federal Trade Commission
David Schmittlein, PhD	John C Head III Dean, MIT Sloan School of Business
Michael Schrage	Research Fellow, MIT Sloan Schools Center for Digital Business
Jeffrey J. Selingo	Contributing Editor, *The Chronicle of Higher Education*, Professor of Practice, Arizona State University
Susan E. Siegel	CEO, GE Ventures, Healthymagination, & Idea Works
Scott Simon	Former Managing Director of PIMCO
Jitendra V. Singh, PhD	Dean, School of Business and Management, Michael Jebsen Professor of Business Chair Professor, Department of Management, Hong Kong University of Science & Technology
Jonathan Spector	President & CEO, The Conference Board
Richard Straub, PhD	President & CEO, Peter Drucker Society Europe, Senior Advisor IBM Global Education Industry, Director of Corporate Services & EU Affairs, EFMD

Kwei Tang, PhD	University Chair Professor and Dean of College of Commerce, National Chengchi University
Rebecca Taylor, PhD	Dean and Professor of Economics, The Open University Business School
Ildiko Tesak, PhD	Founder of OEF of El Salvador
Howard Thomas, PhD	LKCSB Distinguished Term Professor of Strategic Management, Management Education Director, Academic Strategy and Consulting Unit, Singapore Management University
Karl T. Ulrich, ScD	Vice Dean of Innovation and CIBC Professor of Entrepreneurship and e-Commerce, the Wharton School of the University of Pennsylvania
Francisco M. Veloso, PhD	Dean, Catolica-Lisbon School of Business and Economics
N. Venkatraman, PhD	David J. McGrath, Jr. Professor in Management, Boston University Questrom School of Business
Padmasree Warrior	Chief Technology & Strategy Officer, CISCO
David Weil, PhD	Administrator, Wage and Hour Division, United States Department of Labor, Peter and Deborah Wexler Professor of Management, Boston University Questrom School of Business (On Leave)
Peter Wexler	Cofounder, SpiderCloud Wireless
Giselle Weybrecht	Author, *The Sustainable MBA: The Manager's Guide to Green Business*
Marie Wilson, PhD	Pro Vice Chancellor (Business and Law), University of South Australia Business School
Michael Wright	Chief Information Officer, McKinsey & Company

Sri Zaheer, PhD   Dean, Carlson School of Business,
                           University of Minnesota

Lin Zhou, PhD   Dean, Antai College of Economics and
                           Management, Shanghai Jiao
                           Tong University

References

Augier, M., & March, J. G. (2011). *The roots, rituals and rhetorics of change: North American business schools after the second world war*. Stanford, CA: Stanford University Press.

Beer, M. (2001). Why management research findings are unimplementable: An action science perspective. *Reflections: The SoL Journal, 2*(3), 58–65.

Bennis, W. G., & O'Toole, J. (2005). How business schools lost their way. *Harvard Business Review, 83*(5), 96–104.

Bloom, A.-D. (1987). *The closing of the American mind*. New York, NY: Simon and Schuster.

Bok, D. (2003). *Universities in the marketplace: The commercialisation of higher education*. Princeton, NJ: Princeton University Press.

Boland, R. J., Jr, Lyytinen, K., & Yoo, Y. (2007). Wakes of innovation in project networks: The case of digital 3-D representations in architecture, engineering, and construction. *Organization Science, 18*(4), 631–647.

Chesbrough, H. (2003). *Open innovation: The new imperative for creating and profiting from technology*. Cambridge, MA: Harvard Business School Press.

Christensen, C. M., & Carlile, P. R. (2009). Course research: Using the case method to build and teach management theory. *Academy of Management Learning & Education, 8*(2), 240–251.

Christensen, C. M., & Eyring, H. (2011). *The innovative university*. San Francisco, CA: Jossey-Bass.

Corporate Recruiters Survey. Corporate Recruiters Survey 2015 Survey Report. (2015). Retrieved from http://www.gmac.com/market-intelligence-and-research/research-library/employment-outlook/2015-corporate-recruiters-survey-report.aspx

Dash, J. (2000). *The longitude prize*. New York, NY: Frances Foster Books.

Fraguiero, F. (2010). Think locally, but from a global perspective. *Financial Times*, April 26, p. 9.

Fraguiero, F., & Thomas, H. (2011). *Strategic leadership in the business school: Keeping one step ahead*. Cambridge: Cambridge University Press.

Freeman, K. W. (2014). The call for innovation in business education. *People & Strategy, 37*(2), 47–50.

Gallup. (2014). What America needs to know about higher education redesign, February. Gallup, Inc., Washington, DC.

Ghoshal, S. (2005). Bad management theories are destroying good management practices. *Academy of Management Learning & Education*, 4(1), 75–91.

Gordon, R. A., & Howell, J. E. (1959). *Higher education for business*. New York, NY: Columbia University Press.

Iansiti, M., & Lakhani, K. R. (2014). Digital ubiquity: How connections, sensors, and data are revolutionizing business (Digest Summary). *Harvard Business Review*, 92(11), 91–99.

IBM Jam Program Office. (2014, October 7). *Business education jam event summary report*. Unpublished.

IBM Social Insight Group. (2014, July 27). *Boston University pre-jam listening*. Unpublished.

Jaschik, S., & Lederman, D. (Eds.). (2014). *The 2014 inside higher ed survey of college and university chief academic officers*. Washington, DC: Gallup.

Khurana, R. (2007). *From higher aims to hired hands*. Princeton, NJ: Princeton University Press.

King, A., & Lakhani, K. R. (2013). Using open innovation to identify the best ideas. *MIT Sloan Management Review*, 55(1), 41–48.

Kuhlmann, A. (2010). Reinventing innovation. *Ivey Business Journal*, (May–June).

Lakhani, K., & Carlile, P. R. (2010). Myelin repair foundation: Accelerating drug discovery through collaboration. Harvard Business School Technology & Operations Mgt. Unit Case, (610-074).

Lakhani, K. R., & Panetta, J. A. (2007). *The principles of distributed innovation*. Cambridge, MA: MIT Press.

Landry, L. (2014, September 30). *For the next 2 days, thousands will be online discussing the future of business education* [Editorial]. Retrieved from Bostoniano website http://bostinno.streetwise.co/2014/09/30/boston-universitys-online-business-education-jam-future-of-business-education/. Accessed on December 16, 2015.

Mintzberg, H. (2004). *Managers not MBA'S*. London: Pearson Education.

Nuthall, G. (2004). Relating classroom teaching to student learning: A critical analysis of why research has failed to bridge the theory-practice gap. *Harvard educational review*, 74(3), 273–306.

Peters, K., & Thomas, H. (2011). A sustainable model for business schools. *Global Focus*, 5(2), 24–27.

Pew Research. (2013, July). Retrieved from http://www.pewforum.org/2013/07/11/public-esteem-for-military-still-high/

Pfeffer, J., & Fong, C. T. (2002). The end of business schools: Less success than meets the eye. *Academy of Management Learning and Education*, 1(1), 78–95.

Pfeffer, J., & Fong, C. T. (2004). The business school business — Some lessons from the U.S. experience. *Journal of Management Studies*, *41*(8), 1501—1520.

Pierson, F. C. (1959). *The education of American businessmen*. New York, NY: McGraw-Hill.

Reimagining Business Education. (2015, January). *Reimagining business education*. Boston, MA: Boston University Questrom School of Business.

Simon, H. A. (1997). *Administrative behaviour: A study of decision-making processes in administrative organisation*. New York, NY: Free Press.

Skapinker, M. (2011). Why business still ignores business schools. *Financial Times*, January 24.

Tett, G. (2013). The virtual university. *Financial Times*, February 2—3.

The Economist. (2009). A seminal critique of American business education, five decades on [Online extra], *The Economist*, June 4. Retrieved from http://www.economist.com/node/12762453. Accessed on January 7, 2016.

Thomas, H., Lee, M., Thomas, L., & Wilson, A. (2014). *Securing the future of management education: Competitive destruction or constructive innovation* (Vol. 2). Bingley, UK: Emerald Group Publishing Limited.

Thomas, H., Lorange, P., & Sheth, J. (2013, July). *The business school in the twenty-first century: Emergent challenges and new business models*. Cambridge: Cambridge University Press.

Thomas, H., & Peters, K. (2012). A sustainable model for business schools. *Journal of Management Development*, *30*(5), 526—540.

Torvalds, L. B. (1991). What would you like to see most in minix? *Newsgroup: comp.os.minix*, August 26.

Trahan, E. A., & Gitman, L. J. (1995). Bridging the theory-practice gap in corporate finance: A survey of chief financial officers. *The Quarterly Review of Economics and Finance*, *35*(1), 73—87.

Turpin, D. (2013). Challenges and opportunities in the new business education world. *Global Focus*, *7*(2), 8—11.

Upton, D. J. (1999). How can we achieve evidence-based practice if we have a theory—practice gap in nursing today? *Journal of Advanced Nursing*, *29*(3), 549—555.

Westerbeck, T. (2014, September 29). *Business education jam: Let's be cautiously optimistic* [Editorial]. Retrieved from Eduvantis Market Perspectives website http://eduvantis.com/2014/09/29/business-education-jam-cautiously-optimistic/

Whitla, P. (2009). Crowdsourcing and its application in marketing activities. *Contemporary Management Research*, *5*(1), 15—28.